NEW YORK YANKEES

YESTERDAY & TODAY ™

Glenn Stout

Publications International, Ltd.

Glenn Stout has been series editor, since its inception, of the annual anthology *The Best American Sports Writing*. He is the editor or author of more than 60 books, including *Yankees Century*, *Red Sox Century*, *The Dodgers: 120 Years of Dodger Baseball*, and *The Cubs: The Complete Story of Chicago Cubs Baseball*. He lives in Vermont.

Pictured on the front cover, clockwise from top left: Derek Jeter in the final regular season game at old Yankee Stadium, September 21, 2008; Joe DiMaggio, circa 1945; Joe Torre and the Yankees celebrate the 2000 World Series; Yogi Berra and Don Larsen celebrate Larsen's perfect game in the 1956 World Series.

Pictured on the back cover, left to right: Babe Ruth launches another home run; Mariano Rivera shuts down the Texas Rangers on August 7, 2008.

No team in baseball looks forward to Opening Day more than the New York Yankees. Yankee fans have been lucky— for most of the club's history, a pennant and an appearance in the World Series has been a reasonable expectation. From April to October, the Yankees are the center of their universe.

Contents

Yankee scoreboard   page 22

Yankee patch   page 44

Babe Ruth   page 53

Derek Jeter   page 74

Sketchbook   page 86

David Wells   page 138

The New York Yankees

LIKE NO OTHER TEAM IN BASEBALL, the name Yankees conjures up images of places, players, and plays unique to the most successful team in professional sports. One thinks of the Yankees and sees Babe Ruth trotting around the bases, Lou Gehrig standing before a microphone, Joe DiMaggio gliding across center field after a ball in the gap, Mickey Mantle smiling, Derek Jeter racing across the field to snag an errant throw and flip it backhanded toward home, Yankee Stadium draped in bunting, 60,000 fans leaping to their feet to follow the flight of a long fly ball, and a world championship banner ruffling in the breeze on the center-field flagpole.

For over a century the Yankees have been at the epicenter of the great American pastime. No team has been more successful, won more games, or collected more championships. All around the world, the interlocking "NY" has come to symbolize not only the Yankees but America itself.

The Yankees are universal.

This poster touted the 1932 World Series between the Yankees and the Cubs as if it were a prizefight. If baseball were boxing, the Yankees would be heavyweight champions of the world.

The long ball has defined the Yankees. No team in baseball has produced more slugging stars. From Lou Gehrig and Babe Ruth (pictured at left with Miller Huggins) to Alex Rodriguez, whose teammates await him at home plate following a game-winning home run in April 2007 (opposite page), the Bronx Bombers have delivered.

Welcome to Yankee Stadium

THE OLD YANKEE STADIUM was more than a ballpark. It was a museum, a place where baseball history came alive. Some of the greatest games in the history of baseball took place at the stadium in the Bronx. Many of the greatest players the game has ever known called it home.

Pennants are popular fan souvenirs, especially for the Yankees. No team has raised more pennants than the Yankees, and no team has turned more pennants into world championships.

Left: Yankee Stadium may well be the most photographed ballpark in baseball history. Pictured here is Opening Day, 1923. *Right:* Yankee Stadium was the host of more postseason and World Series games than any other ballpark. The stadium and home crowd gave the Yankees a huge advantage over the years.

The Home of the Yankees

SEASON AFTER SEASON, from April to October, ever since it opened in 1923, Yankee Stadium was the center of the baseball universe. Before Yankee Stadium was built, the New York Yankees had never won a World Series. Soon after Yankee Stadium opened, pennants began to fly in the Bronx. Afterward, the Yankees appeared in the World Series 39 times, winning an astounding 26 world championships—more than any other team in major-league baseball.

Yankee Stadium wasn't just a building. It was a living place that changed and evolved over time, a place where yesterday and today met to create a cascade of memories. There are stories everywhere.

Gazing out toward center field one could imagine Joe DiMaggio gracefully chasing after fly balls, earning the nickname "the Yankee Clipper," or see Bernie Williams sliding to make a spectacular catch. The right-field stands were where a fan named Sal Durante caught Roger Maris's 61st home run in 1961 and where 12-year-old Jeffrey Maier helped Derek Jeter's home run over the wall during the 1996 ALCS.

Yankee fans are very loyal to their ballpark. Souvenirs of Yankee Stadium sell well.

When Yankee Stadium first opened, the center-field flagpole was in the field of play, as it was in many ballparks of the era.

Left: Pictured is Opening Day, April 18, 1923. On that day, no one could have imagined that Yankee Stadium would someday become one of New York's most recognizable landmarks. In addition to hosting the Yankees, the stadium served as the home of the football Giants, hosted championship boxing matches, and even served as an open-air church during visits by the Pope.

Below: For more than eight decades, Yankee Stadium was the home of some of the most loyal fans in history. To a young Yankee fan, and even a few older ones, this was the most exciting sight in the world—the exterior of Yankee Stadium just before a ball game.

For much of its history, Yankee Stadium was the biggest ballpark in major-league baseball. This scorecard from 1957 showcases the Yankees' American League pennants.

The unoccupied black seats in center field were where Reggie Jackson spanked his third consecutive home run in Game 6 of the 1977 World Series, and first base is where Lou Gehrig, "the Iron Horse," played during his record-setting 2,130 consecutive games. The pitcher's mound was where catcher Yogi Berra leaped into pitcher Don Larsen's arms to congratulate him after he threw the only perfect game in World Series history in 1956 and where David Wells's teammates lifted him to their shoulders following his perfect game in 1998.

The Yankees celebrated thousands of home runs at home plate, from Babe Ruth's 60th blast in 1927, to Mickey Mantle's final home run in 1968, to Scott Brosius's dramatic, game-tying homer to left in the ninth inning of the fifth game of the 2001 World Series.

Every player who stepped upon the field at Yankee Stadium walked in the footsteps of Yankee legends, and every fan who entered Yankee Stadium knew that he or she was destined to witness history. In Yankee Stadium, like nowhere else, every game of every season had the potential to be absolutely unforgettable.

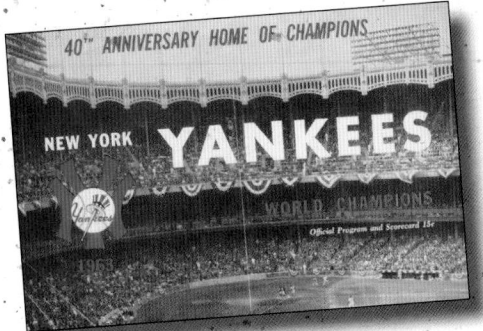

The interior of Yankee Stadium is pictured on this scorecard from 1963, which was the 40th anniversary of Yankee Stadium.

The Big Bat

The New York Yankees have always had "big bats" in their lineup, such as Babe Ruth, Lou Gehrig, Mickey Mantle, Reggie Jackson, and others, but there is only one "Big Bat." Outside the main entrance gate was one of Yankee Stadium's most notable landmarks, a 138-foot-tall replica of a baseball bat, known to everyone as the Big Bat.

Sponsored by the Louisville Slugger bat company, the Big Bat was installed during the 1974–75 renovations. It was a near exact replica of Babe Ruth's bat, and it included a genuine Louisville Slugger trademark, a facsimile of Ruth's signature on the barrel, and even frayed tape around the handle. But the bat wasn't just decorative—it covered an exhaust pipe.

Fans often used the bat as a meeting place before and after games because of its high visibility.

The view from the upper deck of Yankee Stadium offered perhaps the best view of the ballpark.

Before Construction

The site that would one day be occupied by Yankee Stadium was, appropriately enough, a lumberyard. In the ensuing decades, the Yankees would become known for the way they used their own lumber to blast home run after home run.

Prior to the building of Yankee Stadium, the ten-acre property between 158th and 161st Street was owned by the estate of William Waldorf Astor, one of New York's most prominent and wealthy citizens. A lumberyard held a lease on much of the property, and the rest, which had once been a farm, was partially surrounded by a ramshackle fence. The lot was strewn with trash and covered by weeds. The Harlem River lay only a few hundred feet to the west.

Yankee fans were already familiar with the location. The Polo Grounds, home of the National League New York Giants and since 1913 the temporary home of the Yankees, was located directly across the river. In future years, on the rare occasions when both parks were being used at the same time, fans at the Polo Grounds could hear the crowd cheering in Yankee Stadium.

This lumberyard in Washington Heights was the site of the Yankees' first home. Known by most fans as "Hilltop Park," the official name of the park was more mundane: American League Park.

From 1913 through 1922, the Yankees were tenants of the National League New York Giants at the Polo Grounds. Slugger Babe Ruth said he preferred hitting at the Polo Grounds, where the fence down the right-field line was only 258 feet away.

Yankee Stadium and the Polo Grounds sat on opposite sides of the Harlem River. At times it was even possible to hear the crowd from one park while at the other.

Building Yankee Stadium

Yankee Stadium was designed by the Osborne Engineering Company. As originally conceived, a vast, triple-decked grandstand was to have surrounded the entire field. But that was never built.

The Yankees insisted that the stadium be finished by Opening Day in 1923, and for that reason the original plans were scaled back. The triple-decked grandstand stopped short of the outfield. A single deck extended into left field and wooden bleachers surrounded the remainder of the outfield. Construction began on May 5, 1922, and would cost $2.5 million.

More than 45,000 cubic yards of earth had to be removed to prepare the site. Construction of the stadium required 20,000 yards of concrete, 800 tons of reinforced steel, and 2,200 tons of structural steel. Thirteen thousand yards of topsoil were trucked in to cover the field, and 16,000 square feet of sod was planted. Only 287 days after breaking ground, Yankee Stadium opened on April 18, 1923. Appropriately enough, the Yankees beat the Red Sox 4–1 as Babe Ruth hit the first home run in the stadium that sportswriter Fred Lieb dubbed the "House that Ruth Built."

Shortly after the turn of the century, ballpark designers abandoned wood for steel and concrete construction. This allowed for a much larger grandstand.

Above: The trademark frieze along the upper deck of Yankee Stadium disappeared during the 1974–75 renovation. The feature was resurrected for new Yankee Stadium.
Left: Stadium designers were optimistic when they installed a warning track around the outfield. At its deepest point, in left-center field, the fence was originally 500 feet from home plate.

Renovation of Yankee Stadium

ONLY A FEW HOURS after Yankee first baseman Mike Hegan hit a fly ball to end the 1973 season, demolition and construction crews moved into Yankee Stadium. At the age of 50, Yankee Stadium needed a facelift. For the next two years, while the Yankees played home games in Queens at the Mets' home park, Shea Stadium, the "House that Ruth Built" underwent a complete renovation.

At the cost of approximately $100 million, workers stripped the ballpark down to its bones, leaving little more than the steel frame of the grandstand and the concrete risers. The concrete facade atop the grandstand was removed, as were all the old wood and iron seats.

All 118 steel columns that supported the upper deck were removed, and the deck was cantilevered, allowing fans an unobstructed view. The field itself was reconfigured, retaining the same basic shape but reducing the distance to the outfield fence in center field and left-center while slightly increasing the distance down each foul line. The monuments in center field were relocated out of the field of play, and new 22-inch-wide plastic seats replaced the original 18-inch-wide wooden seats. This reduced seating capacity from almost 70,000 to 55,000.

After the renovation, which included updating and modernizing many interior features, Yankee Stadium still evoked the original ballpark.

Midway through the renovation, in April 1975, cranes and trucks are scattered across the field that was home to the Yankee Clipper and the Iron Horse, Joe DiMaggio and Lou Gehrig.

Yankee shortstop Phil Rizzuto surveys the field he called home during his storied career.

New Yankee Stadium

ON AUGUST 16, 2006, just one block north of Yankee Stadium, the Yankees broke ground on the construction of their new home, ensuring that the Yankees would play ball in the Bronx well into the 21st century. Although the stadium is new, the Yankees did not abandon Yankee Stadium—they just rebuilt it. New Yankee Stadium includes parts of both the original stadium and the 1974–75 renovation, ensuring that all the best qualities of Yankee Stadium remain in place.

When fans arrive at new Yankee Stadium for the first time, they feel as if they are traveling back in time. From the outside, the new stadium features an exterior facade almost identical to that of the original Yankee Stadium, and the roof of the grandstand is adorned with the same signature frieze and copper latticework that decorated the original Yankee Stadium. Inside they enjoy larger concourses, a wider variety of concessions, and more comfortable seating. When Derek Jeter jogs out to play shortstop in new Yankee Stadium, however, he feels right at home. The field of play is

The Yankees spent more than $1 billion of their own money on the new Yankee Stadium. They hope to recoup much of that money with the "great hall," an enormous shopping area inside the stadium.

the exact same size and shape as it is today, and the new stadium seats 51,000 fans.

The Yankees were scheduled to make history in new Yankee Stadium on April 16, 2009. As Derek Jeter said at a press conference on June 15, 2005, when the Yankees first announced their plans, "There are a lot of good memories here. Now we'll try to take them across the street."

Yankee owner George Stein-brenner and New York Mayor Michael Bloomberg shared the spotlight at groundbreaking ceremonies for the new park. Note the ceremonial shovels, which had handles made of baseball bats.

Early Fans

When Yankee Stadium first opened, attending a Yankee game was almost a formal event. Games usually started in midafternoon, and during the week most fans were businessmen who left work a few hours early. Nearly everyone wore a suit and hat. Female fans were rare.

Most working people could attend games only on the weekend. Then entire families often made their way to the park. As a result, weekend crowds were usually bigger, with more women and children, and the fans were louder and more involved with the game.

New York is a city of immigrants. In the early days of Yankee Stadium, many immigrants learned the game of baseball in the stands at Yankee Stadium. The neighborhood around Yankee Stadium was predominantly Italian, and Italian fans turned out in large numbers to see Italian-American stars Tony Lazzeri and Joe DiMaggio play for the Yankees.

In fact, the Italian-American crowds at Yankee Stadium are responsible for one of the most famous nicknames in baseball. They loved Babe Ruth and called him the Italian word for baby—"Bambino."

Above: Babe Ruth hands out candy bars to fans in the right-field bleachers before a game in 1928. *Left:* Perhaps this fan, attending a game in 1950, tired of the way the Yankees rolled over most of their opponents. Everyone else still seems interested in the game's outcome.

Fans Today

There is no such thing as a "typical" Yankee fan. Today the crowd at Yankee Stadium looks like New York. Fans of all persuasions—young and old, rich and poor, male and female, African-American, Caucasian, Latino, Asian, and everything in between—turn out and come together to root for the Yankees. Perhaps no other sports facility in the United States draws a more diverse and cosmopolitan crowd.

The luxury box seats near the dugouts and behind home plate are often occupied by celebrities and other well-known New Yorkers, including former Mayor Rudy Giuliani, real estate developer Donald Trump, and actor Billy Crystal. But Yankee Stadium isn't just for the rich and famous.

Out in the bleachers, the self-described "bleacher creatures" are the Yankees' most rabid and raucous fans. They are almost a part of the game. They "call out" each Yankee starting player, chanting each name and clapping in rhythm until the player acknowledges them.

Actor Denzel Washington proudly wears his Yankee cap while attending the 2001 World Series with musician Lenny Kravitz.

Former president Bill Clinton enjoys a game in 2005 with Yankee owner George Steinbrenner and former Dodger manager Tommy Lasorda. The Yankees presented Clinton with a $1 million check for tsunami relief.

The "bleacher creatures" enjoy their moment in the spotlight as they call out Yankee players at the beginning of each game. Many of these fans attend every game, every season, and have developed lifelong friendships that span generations and cross cultural and ethnic barriers.

The Original Monuments

Yankee catcher Bill Dickey (left) and manager Joe McCarthy (right) unveil the memorial to Lou Gehrig on July 6, 1941. Gehrig passed away earlier that season.

Babe Ruth's widow, Claire, unveils Ruth's monument on April 19, 1949. Wreaths are placed on Gehrig's and Huggins's monuments.

Near the end of the 1929 season, Yankee manager Miller Huggins passed away. On May 30, 1932, the Yankees unveiled a monument to Huggins, a brass plaque mounted on a red granite rectangular cube, which was placed deep in left-center field near the flagpole.

Following the death of first baseman Lou Gehrig in 1941, the Yankees built a similar monument to Gehrig and placed it alongside Huggins's monument. After Babe Ruth died in 1948, the Yankees unveiled a monument to Ruth, placing it on the other side of Huggins, flanking the manager's monument with those of his two favorite players. Later, the Yankees installed plaques honoring owner Jacob Ruppert, general manager Ed Barrow, and outfielders Joe DiMaggio and Mickey Mantle on the outfield wall behind the monuments.

All three monuments, as well as the Yankee Stadium flagpole and the plaques, were in the field of play. On rare occasions, a batted ball reached the monuments, forcing outfielders to weave between the monuments while retrieving the ball. Once, when a Yankee outfielder fumbled for the ball amid the monuments, Yankee manager Casey Stengel called out, "Ruth, Gehrig, Huggins, *somebody* get that ball back to the infield!"

The monuments and flagpole were in the field of play, and as demonstrated by this photo, outfielders sometimes had to play the ball from behind the monuments. Fortunately (or unfortunately), few batters hit the ball that far.

Monument Park

DURING THE RENOVATION of 1974–75, the Yankee Stadium outfield was made smaller. Instead of leaving the monuments in the field of play, the Yankees created Monument Park beyond the left-center field fence near where the monuments were originally built. The park was open before every Yankee game and also included in tours of the stadium.

The monuments to Huggins, Gehrig, and Ruth are the centerpieces of Monument Park, which also includes a wall bearing plaques honoring DiMaggio, Mantle, Barrow, and Ruppert. Over time, the Yankees have chosen to commemorate other great figures in Yankee history in Monument Park, adding plaques to honor people such as the first African-American to play for the Yankees, catcher Elston Howard; managers Billy Martin and Joe McCarthy; broadcaster Mel Allen; public address announcer Bob Sheppard; and many others. There are also smaller mounted plaques honoring each Yankee to have his number retired.

The most recent monument was dedicated to the victims of the 9/11 attacks at the World Trade Center. All monuments and plaques were relocated to Monument Park in new Yankee Stadium.

Following the 1974–75 renovation, all the monuments and plaques were moved into Monument Park beyond the left-field fence.

When visiting Yankee Stadium, many opposing players make a pilgrimage to Monument Park. Here Arizona Diamondback first baseman Mark Grace makes a visit during the 2001 World Series.

Construction workers admire the Babe Ruth monument after transporting it to the new Yankee Stadium in February 2009.

Old Scoreboard

THE ORIGINAL SCOREBOARD at Yankee Stadium was one of a kind. Towering several stories high and more than 150 feet wide, the manually operated scoreboard loomed over the bleachers in right-center field. There was room on the massive board for the line scores of every game in the major leagues, the batting order of both the Yankees and their opponents, the number of the player at bat, the ball/strike count, the number of outs, the identity of the umpires, and the time of the game the next day.

Perhaps the most striking feature was the art deco scoreboard clock, sponsored by the Longines watch company, that for years sat atop the scoreboard. The scoreboard also included ten electronic speakers on top of the board and two on each side to broadcast public address announcements.

In 1946, partially electronic, field-level, auxiliary scoreboards were added along the fence in both right- and left-center field. And in 1959, the main scoreboard was electrified and redesigned as the Yankees unveiled major league's first electronic message board. In 1961, as Roger Maris pursued Babe Ruth's home run record, the Yankees used the message board to keep a count of Maris's home runs.

The old scoreboard towered over center field in Yankee Stadium. Not only were the lineups of both teams on display, but so was the score of every game being played that day.

Over time, the scoreboard evolved as advertisers such as Ballantine Beer and the Longines watch company became sponsors.

Each picture of the scoreboard is a snapshot of history. This image was taken at the top of the fifth inning on October 1, 1961. Moments earlier, in the fourth inning, Roger Maris hit his record 61st home run of the season.

Going Electric

By the 1970s, the old scoreboard was an anachronism. A spate of new ballparks featured more interactive, electronic scoreboards. The old scoreboard would disappear during the 1974–75 renovation.

DURING THE 1974-75 renovation, the old scoreboard was dismantled and replaced by the largest scoreboard in professional sports. Stretching across the outfield from one side of the stadium to the other, the 560-foot-long scoreboard included baseball's very first "telescreen," allowing the Yankees to display high-quality photographs and video. Completely electronic, the scoreboard originally included three separate electronic displays separated by advertising billboards.

Like the original scoreboard, the new scoreboard evolved over time. The electronic display allowed the Yankees to change advertisements in an instant. In 1983, the telescreen was replaced with a color "Diamond Vision" video screen. In 2002, that screen was replaced and upgraded. The new screen, measuring 25×33 feet, was installed using a crane.

Of course, the new Yankee Stadium includes an even more magnificent video display. The Diamond Vision scoreboard is a monster, measuring 100.8 feet wide and 58.8 feet tall. It also includes the latest technology, resulting in incredibly sharp and vibrant images. While the old stadium's scoreboard included 486,400 LED lamps, the new one contains more than 8.6 million. Now that's hi-def!

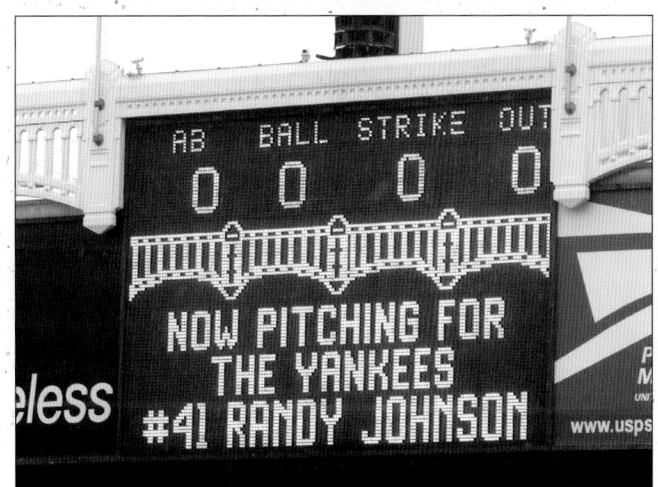

The new scoreboard displayed pictures and video, and it could also provide fans with background information on players and alert them to important milestones.

Yankee Juggernauts

IN MANY SEASONS the Yankees' only competition has been their own history. No other team in baseball has been more successful. Season after season, decade after decade, they have set the standard. The Yankees are the touchstone against which every other franchise in professional sports measures success.

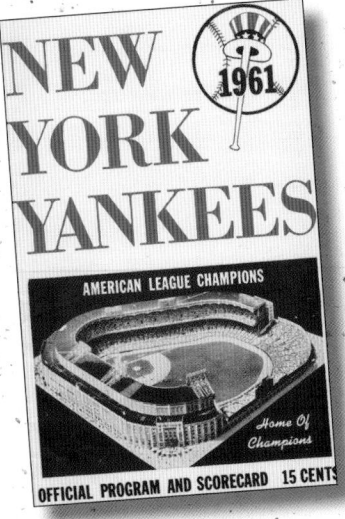

The Yankees have never been shy about touting their own performance, as on this scorecard from 1961 that refers to Yankee Stadium as the "Home of Champions." In many seasons, such hyperbole hasn't been bragging but a simple declaration of fact.

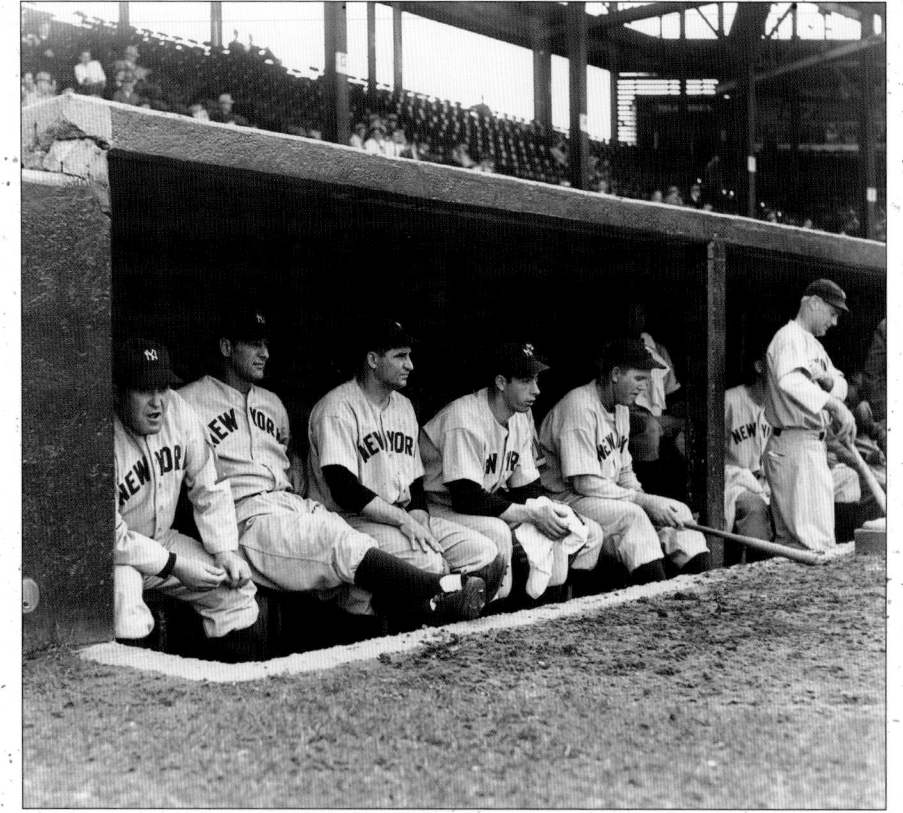

Left: Which Yankee team was the greatest? Some would say the 1936 Yankees, which featured manager Joe McCarthy (left), Lou Gehrig (second from left), and Joe DiMaggio (center). Or was it the 1927 team, the 1961 Bronx Bombers, or the 1998 club? The argument has no definitive answer, but Yankee fans love to discuss it anyway. *Right:* This may well be a Yankee fan's favorite scene—the Yankees on the field after the last out celebrating a victory in the postseason. Here the Yankees celebrate their victory over Cleveland in the 1998 ALCS.

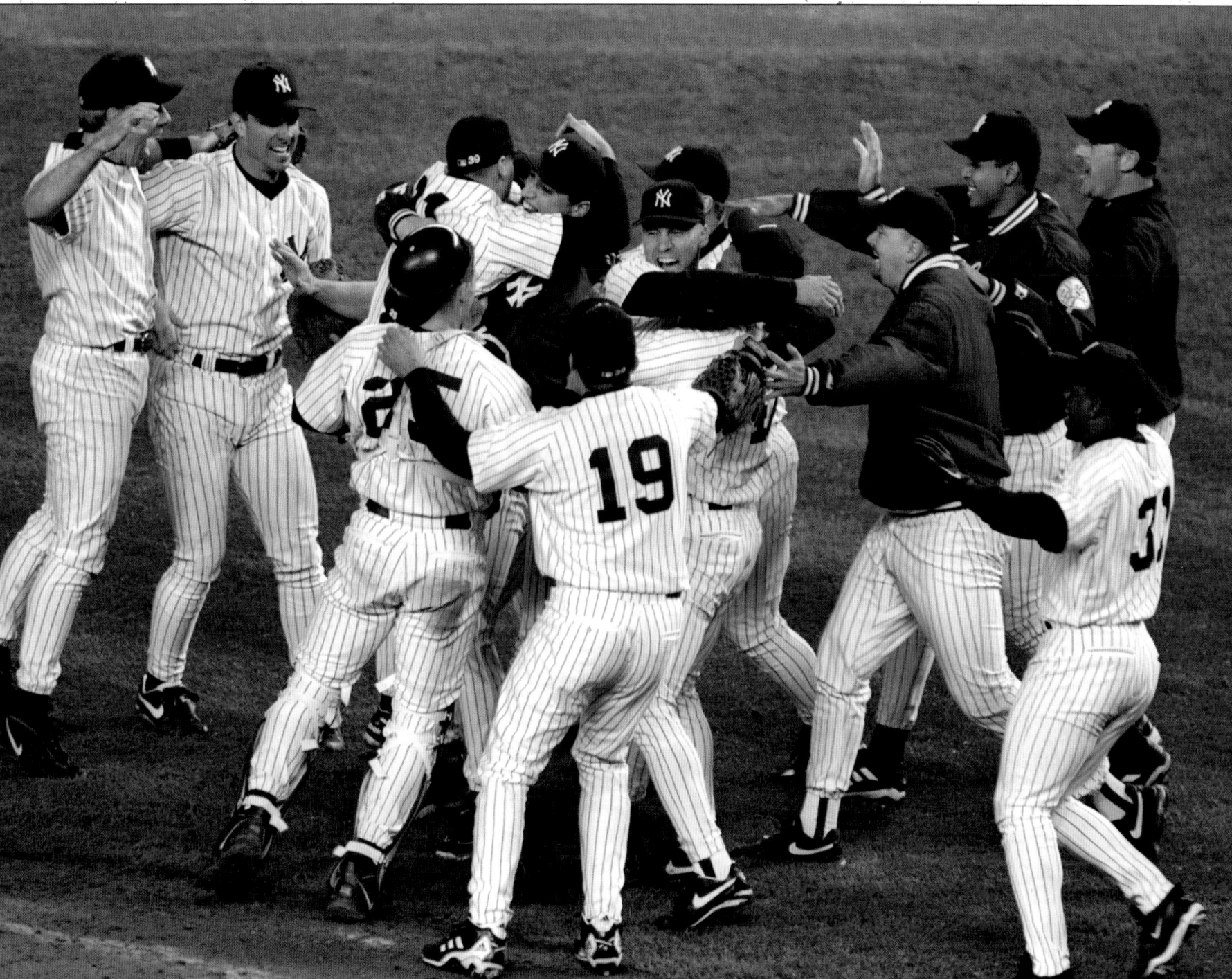

1904: One Pitch Away

92–59   .609 $-1^{1}/_{2}$

In 1904, New York pitcher Jack Chesbro used the spitball to forge perhaps the single greatest season any major-league pitcher has ever had. Unfortunately, after throwing 454 innings in 1904, Chesbro's arm was never the same and he was out of the big leagues by 1909.

WHEN HE CREATED the Yankees (then known as the Highlanders) in 1903, American League president Ban Johnson promised Yankee owners Frank Farrell and William Devery that he would help stock the club with star players. By 1904, Johnson's promise was fulfilled.

Wee Willie Keeler followed his adage to "hit 'em where they ain't" to perfection, batting .343 for the season. In the middle of the year, Johnson arranged the trade of Boston outfielder Patsy Dougherty to New York, filling a hole in the Highlander outfield. Manager Clark Griffith and his club soon found themselves in their first pennant race.

No one was more responsible than pitcher Jack Chesbro, one of the first to use the spitball. Hitters found Chesbro's pitch almost impossible to hit. He set the modern major-league record for victories in a single season with an incredible 41.

To win the pennant, New York needed Chesbro to win 42 games. On the last day of the season, New York needed to sweep Boston in a doubleheader to win the pennant. But in the final inning of the first game, one of Chesbro's spitballs slipped from his grip. That wild pitch delivered the pennant to Boston.

Left: Right fielder Wee Willie Keeler was the Yankees' first star. During their inaugural season, a deep hole in right field at the Yankees home park was known as "Keeler's Hollow." *Above:* The trade of outfielder Patsy Dougherty from Boston to New York for Bob Unglaub in 1904 was the first big trade between the two clubs. Dougherty hit .283 for New York and helped the club challenge Boston for the pennant.

27

1927: The Greatest Team

110–44 .714 +19

THE 1927 YANKEES were revolutionary. They were the first team to feature two great home run hitters and make use of a relief ace. The result was the best baseball team in history at the time. They were a club that didn't just win, they won big, scoring runs in bunches and shutting down the opposition's offense. No one who saw them had ever seen anything like it before.

At the start of the 1927 season, manager Miller Huggins changed the batting order and moved first baseman Lou Gehrig up in the batting order from fifth to fourth, just behind Babe Ruth. The results were dramatic as the two sluggers created the most devastating combination in baseball history. Ruth hit a record 60 home runs and Gehrig, in his first great season, added 47. That was more than twice as many as any two players had ever hit in combination before. They keyed a Yankee offense that scored a record 975 runs.

Yet the Yankees didn't always need to score big to win. Paced by Waite Hoyt's 22 victories, the pitching staff was the best in baseball. On the rare occasion the starters faltered, Huggins called on sidearm relief

ace Wilcy Moore. The rubber-armed sinkerball pitcher appeared in 50 games, pitching over 200 innings, winning 19 games, and saving 13.

No other team had a chance. The Yankees won the pennant by 19 games and then beat the Pittsburgh Pirates—a team with three future Hall of Famers in the starting lineup—in four straight games to win the World Series. The Yankees outscored the Pirates 23–10.

Manager Miller Huggins had the task of taking a group of stars and turning them into a team. He did his job to perfection.

Left: Waite Hoyt (pictured) may have led the staff with 22 victories, but Wilcy Moore and Herb Pennock both won 19, Urban Shocker won 18, and Dutch Ruether chipped in with another 13 victories. Bob Shawkey, at 2–3, was the only Yankee pitcher below .500. *Below:* A scorecard from the 1927 season. Despite never being challenged for the pennant, the Yankees topped the 1 million mark for eight seasons out of nine, leading the major leagues in attendance.

Eighty years after they last stepped onto the field, many consider the 1927 Yankees the greatest team of all time. They possessed a near perfect blend of power, pitching, and defense.

Paced by Lou Gehrig, Bill Dickey, and rookie Joe DiMaggio, the 1936 Yankees sported one of the most potent lineups in baseball history.

1936: Good and Getting Better

102–51   .667   +19.5

ENTERING THE 1936 SEASON, the Yankees, with Lou Gehrig at first base, Bill Dickey behind the plate, and Red Rolfe at third base, were already very good. Then rookie outfielder Joe DiMaggio joined the team. Yankee fans had a new hero, and the club went from good to great.

DiMaggio began the season on the bench with an injury. But after he made his first appearance on May 3, the 1936 Yankees became perhaps the greatest offensive team in baseball history. One week after DiMaggio joined the team, the Yankees moved into first place and slowly pulled away from the rest of the league. The Yankees beat the other teams into submission, scoring 10 or more runs an astounding 41 times. Six players in the starting lineup hit over .300, five knocked in more than 100 runs, and the Yankees hit .300 as a team. Bill Dickey hit .362, and Lou Gehrig earned the MVP Award by hitting 49 home runs with 152 RBI. DiMaggio? He hit .323 with 29 home runs in his rookie season.

New York clinched the pennant on September 9, the earliest date ever at the time. They finished 19½ games ahead of the Detroit Tigers, then they beat the New York Giants in the World Series in six games.

Third baseman Red Rolfe anchored the Yankee infield of Lou Gehrig, shortstop Frank Crosetti, and second baseman Tony Lazzeri.

Bill Dickey had the pleasure of catching the league's best pitching staff. Seven Yankee pitchers won nine or more games in 1936.

Above: Joe DiMaggio was a star from the first time he appeared in the lineup. He began the season in right field before moving to center field after Myril Hoag fractured his skull in an outfield collision. *Left:* Fans filling in their scorecards wore out their pencils on the 1936 Yankees; the team scored a record 1,065 runs.

1947: Back to Normal

97–57   .630   +12

U NDER NEW MANAGER Bucky Harris, the Yankees, who had last won a pennant in 1943, resumed their customary perch atop the American League. But it wasn't easy. They weren't the same team of stars they were before the war; they were a ballclub made up of solid veterans and a few prize youngsters.

Joe DiMaggio missed the start of the season as he recovered from heel surgery, and as late as mid-May, the Yankees were below .500. Then DiMaggio returned and got hot. And when DiMaggio started hitting, the Yankees started winning.

In midseason it all came together. Paced by starting pitcher Allie Reynolds, rookie Spec Shea, and fireballing reliever Joe Page, the Yankee pitching staff gave the league's best offense some help.

Beginning on June 29, the Yankees won 19 straight games. At the end of the streak, they led the Detroit Tigers by 11½ games and had the pennant in their back pocket.

The Yankees clinched first place on September 15, and they defeated the Dodgers in the World Series.

Above: This scorecard came in handy in 1947, because after the war, the phrase "you can't tell the players without a scorecard" rang true. Rookies and other young-sters joined veterans returning from combat to lead the Yankees into a new era. *Above right:* Fireballer Allie Reynolds emerged as the staff ace in 1947. Reynolds, who was a quarter Native American, came to the Yankees in a deal that sent Joe Gordon to the Cleveland Indians in 1946.

Manager Bucky Harris (left) won a pennant in 1947, his first season as Yankee skipper. But when Cleveland manager Lou Boudreau (right) led the Indians to the pennant in 1948, Harris was let go.

Relief pitcher Joe Page made 54 relief appearances in 1947, and statisticians later determined that he led the league with 17 saves.

A sure sign of normalcy at the end of World War II was the return of the Yankees to the World Series in 1947. Although the club was led by veterans Phil Rizzuto and Joe DiMaggio, rookies, including Yogi Berra, played key roles in the championship.

The 1956 Yankees won the pennant and the World Series with power, cracking 190 home runs as a team and serving notice that with Mickey Mantle in the lineup, the Bronx Bombers would live up to their reputation.

1956: Power Plus

97–57   .630   +9

AT AGE 24, Mickey Mantle was the best player in baseball, hitting .353 with 52 home runs. Almost by himself, he made the Yankees the best team in the game.

On Opening Day in Washington, Mantle hit two of the longest home runs of his career and never looked back. The Yankees took command of the pennant race in mid-May and were never challenged.

It almost didn't seem fair. Even if the opposition managed to get Mantle out, catcher Yogi Berra, outfielder Hank Bauer, and first baseman Bill Skowron all enjoyed superb seasons. And on the rare occasion another team was able to shut the Yankees down, they still had a hard time scoring against the youthful Yankee pitching staff. Whitey Ford, at age 27, was the old man of the Yankee rotation. He won 19 games, and Johnny Kucks, only 22, added 18 wins of his own.

New York won the pennant by nine games and capped the season off by beating the Dodgers in the World Series.

Right: Pictured from left to right are Mickey Mantle, Casey Stengel, Yogi Berra, and Hank Bauer. Ex-marine Bauer's 26 home runs in 1956 were third on the team after Mantle and Berra.

Top: After falling to the Dodgers in the 1955 World Series, the Yankees exacted revenge in 1956, taking the Series in seven games. Here the club celebrates after the final out in Game 7. *Above:* A bat engraved with Yogi Berra's and Bill "Moose" Skowron's signatures. Skowron's big bat accounted for 90 RBI in 1956.

1961: Making History

109–53 .673 +8

IN 1961, Roger Maris hit third in the Yankee lineup. Mickey Mantle batted cleanup. Together the "M&M Boys" hit 115 home runs and powered the Yankees to a pennant.

Yankee scorecards didn't tell the whole story of Roger Maris's amazing 1961 season. Maris hit 31 of his 61 home runs on the road.

Believe it or not, the Yankees actually got off to a slow start. Beginning on May 17, however, Maris hit 23 home runs in his next 36 games as the Yankees surged into first place by winning 23 of 36, putting away the pennant.

For the rest of the year, the only question that mattered was whether or not Maris or Mantle would break Babe Ruth's home run record. Maris won that race, hitting his 61st home run on the last day of the season. Mantle, hampered by injuries, finished with "only" 54 home runs.

The Yankees won the pennant by 8 games, winning 109 regular-season games. Then they beat the Reds in the World Series.

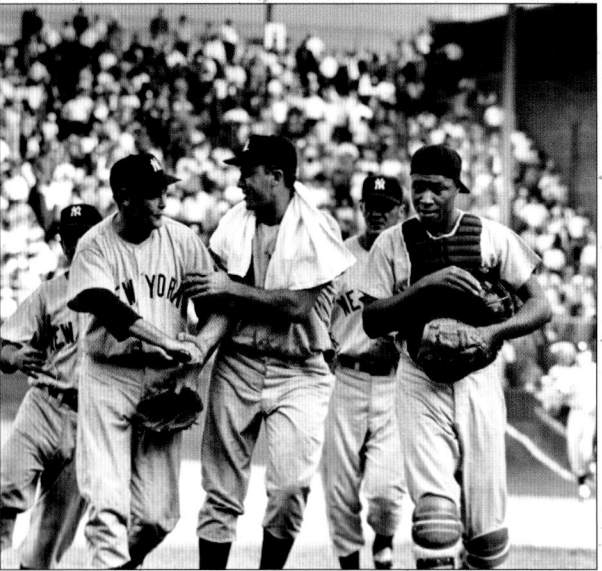

Above: Roger Maris's swing was made for Yankee Stadium. In contrast to sluggers such as Ruth and Mantle, who hit tape-measure home runs, Maris was a dead pull hitter who hit line drives that dropped just over the fence. *Left:* The Yankees blitzed the Reds in five games to win the 1961 World Series. Pitcher Bud Daley (at left with glove) is congratulated by John Blanchard. Bill Skowron (behind), and Elston Howard (right) walk off the field after winning the Series.

How good were the 1961 Yankees? The Detroit Tigers won 101 games and still finished in second place, eight games behind New York. Although Mickey Mantle and Roger Maris received all the headlines, nearly every player on the roster enjoyed a career year.

The members of the Bronx Zoo. The 1977 and 1978 Yankees marked a return to glory for the franchise. For the first time in a generation, the Yankees mattered again.

1978: The Comeback

100–63   .613   +1

For the first half of the 1978 season, the Yankees were a mess. As manager Billy Martin warred with slugger Reggie Jackson and pitcher Catfish Hunter battled a sore arm, the Boston Red Sox bolted out to an enormous lead. On July 17, the Yankees trailed Boston by 14 long games.

Martin resigned a few days later and was replaced by Bob Lemon. Almost overnight, the Yankees turned their season around.

Jackson and everyone else started hitting, and pitcher Ron Guidry, on his way to a 25–3 record, was magnificent. In early September, the Yankees went into Boston trailing by four games. Four days later, they left tied for the division lead after beating Boston four times in what the press called "the Boston Massacre."

The two clubs ended the season tied, but the Yankees won the playoff on Bucky Dent's three-run home run. In the postseason, they beat the Kansas City Royals to win the pennant, and then they defeated the Dodgers to win the World Series.

Catfish Hunter returned to form late in the season to help spark the Yankees to a pennant.

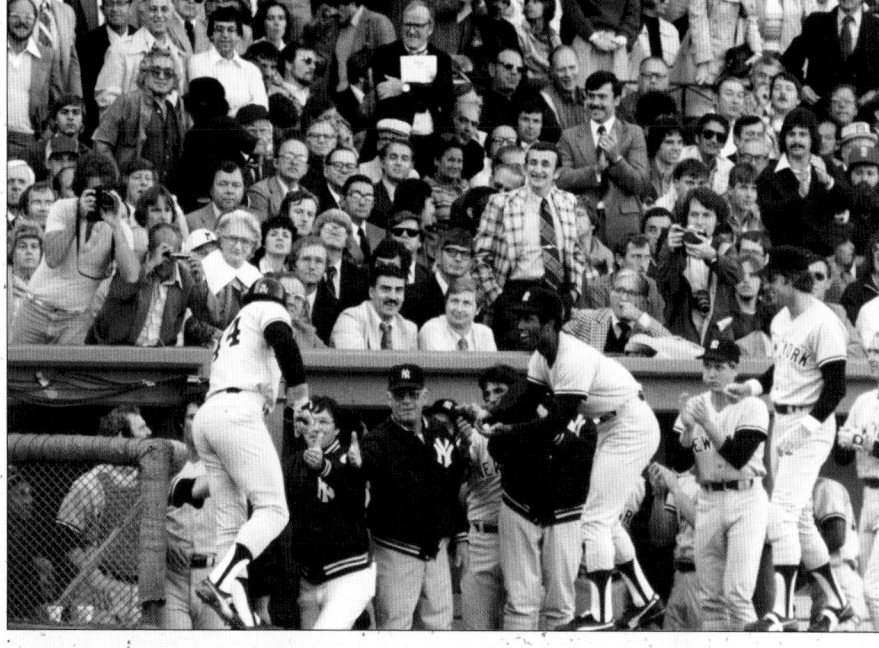

Above: The pennant race between the Yankees and Boston in 1978 reignited baseball's best rivalry. Here Reggie Jackson returns to the dugout after hitting a home run in Fenway Park.
Left: On the rare occasion that Ron Guidry (left) faltered, Goose Gossage (right) backed him up. The two pitchers combined to beat the Red Sox in the playoff game in Boston.

1980: A Steady Course

103–59 .636 +3

Aafter tumbling to fourth place in 1979 in a season marred by the death of captain Thurman Munson, the Yankees fired manager Billy Martin and replaced him with coach Dick Howser. After the temperamental Martin, Howser's steady hand and low-key approach was just what the team needed.

The team thrived under the new manager. Reggie Jackson responded with the best season of his Yankee career, hitting .300 with 41 home runs and hustling all season. Young Rick Cerone filled in admirably behind the plate and veteran sinkerball pitcher Tommy John won 22 games.

On the rare occasion the starting pitching faltered, the Yankees had an answer. Pitcher Ron Davis emerged as the best middleman in baseball, and Rich Gossage slammed the door in the eighth and the ninth.

The Yankees moved into first place on May 14, and despite a late charge by the Baltimore Orioles, the Yankees won 103 games to win the division by three games. Unfortunately, they fell to the Royals in the playoffs. After winning the AL pennant the next year, they would not make another postseason appearance for more than a decade.

Hopes were high when the 1980 yearbook was written. But despite trading first baseman Chris Chambliss for pitcher Tom Underwood and catcher Rick Cerone and signing pitcher Rudy May and first baseman Bob Watson as free agents, the 1980 Yankees fell short—losing in the playoffs to Kansas City.

Left: Hard-throwing relief pitcher Ron Davis served as set-up man for closer Goose Gossage. *Below:* Tommy John won 22 games and anchored the Yankee pitching staff in 1980. His career appeared to be over in 1974, before Dr. Frank Jobe performed experimental surgery on his elbow, transplanting a ligament, in what is now popularly known as "Tommy John" surgery.

The 1980 Yankees won 103 games, the most regular-season victories by a Yankee team since 1963. Not until 1998 would another Yankee team win more.

Before the start of the season, no one predicted that the 1998 Yankees would win more games than any team in club history. Every player on the roster contributed to the Yankees' 114 wins.

1998: A New Standard

114–48   .704   +22

THE YANKEES HAD only one win five games into the 1998 season. There was already speculation that George Steinbrenner would fire manager Joe Torre.

The next day, Torre managed like it was Game 7 of the World Series, and the Yankees emerged with a hard-fought 13–7 victory. They then won 16 of their next 18 games and moved into first place on April 30. But they were just getting started.

The 1998 Yankees were not a team of super performers. No one hit more than 28 home runs or hit higher than .339, and only pitcher David Cone won 20 games. They were, however, a team without a weakness. Every player on the roster, from starting right fielder Paul O'Neill to backup infielder Homer Bush to closer Mariano Rivera, simply did his job day in and day out.

By June 1, the Yankees already led the division by 7½ games. A few days later, Cuban pitcher Orlando Hernandez joined the club and the Yankees got even better. Despite a late-season slump, the Yankees still won the most games in team history: 114. They

charged through the playoffs on their way to a world championship, winning 11 postseason contests and losing only twice.

The 1927 Yankees finally had some competition.

Manager Joe Torre (left) was the perfect man to lead the 1998 Yankees, teaching a group of stars to play as a team. Here Torre celebrates the World Series victory with George Steinbrenner.

Above: Orlando Hernandez, "El Duque," pitched his first game in pinstripes on June 3, 1998. He led the Yankees to a 7–1 win over the Devil Rays, and the Yankees rarely lost when he was on the mound. *Left:* Outfielder Paul O'Neill was acquired from the Cincinnati Reds after the 1992 season in exchange for Roberto Kelly. O'Neill thrived in New York, and fans appreciated his intense, hard-nosed approach and clutch hitting.

2003: The Better Team

101–61   **.623**   **+6**

I N THE 2003 SEASON it seemed as if the baseball universe contained only two teams, the Yankees and their archrivals the Boston Red Sox. Under new ownership, the Red Sox took direct aim at the Yankees.

Although the rivalry between the two clubs was already the best in baseball, it reached a fever pitch in 2003 when the Yankees outbid the Red Sox for Cuban pitcher Jose Contreras. Red Sox president Larry Lucchino called the Yankees the "evil empire," and the battle was on.

Victory went to the Yankees. Boston stalked the Yankees all year long, but New York simply had too much firepower for the Sox. The Yankees clubbed 230 home runs, and Contreras came on in midseason to win seven games and make an already good team even better. An eight-game winning streak in September helped put Boston away. New York won the division with 101 victories, but the Red Sox still earned the wild-card berth.

The two teams were destined to meet in the playoffs, and they played a thrilling seven-game series that ended with Aaron Boone's walk-off home run as the better team won in baseball's biggest rivalry.

After taking a two games to one lead in the World Series against Florida, the Yankees lost three straight, including Game 6, which the owner of this ticket watched in person. Marlins pitcher Josh Beckett hurled a shutout to beat the Yankees 2–0.

It seemed as if Game 7 of the 2003 ALCS between the Yankees and Red Sox might never end. But in the bottom of the 11th inning, Yankee third baseman Aaron Boone cracked a leadoff home run off Boston pitcher Tim Wakefield to win the game and the series for the Yankees.

The club's 100th anniversary proved to be a marketing bonanza, with even non-Yankee fans buying merchandise, including patches as shown.

Relief pitcher Mariano Rivera was his usual spectacular self during the 2003 regular season, saving 40 games with a 1.66 ERA. Here Joe Torre congratulates him after a save.

After thumping the Red Sox in the playoffs, the 2003 Yankees seemed likely to go down in history as one of the franchise's best teams. They fell to the Florida Marlins, however, in the World Series. Here Hideki Matsui congratulates his teammates after they won Game 2 of the Series.

Casey Stengel or Joe Torre?

THE TWO BEST Yankee managers since World War II have a lot in common. When each man was hired, all the experts thought it was a mistake.

When Casey Stengel was hired by the Yankees in 1949, most observers thought it was a joke. Stengel had a reputation of being an entertaining clown and had failed in two stints as a big-league manager with the Dodgers and Braves.

Although Joe Torre had been somewhat more successful as manager of the Braves, Mets, and Cardinals, he was still considered a failure. The headline of one New York tabloid described him as "Clueless Joe."

Yet both managers proved the critics wrong. The veteran leaders had nothing to lose and weren't afraid of being fired. Each had the self-confidence to follow his own instincts and act decisively.

But who is the better manager, Casey or Joe?

Based on their records alone, the pick is a toss-up. In Stengel's 12 seasons, the Yankees won 10 pennants and 7 world titles. During Stengel's first five seasons as manager, the Yankees won the world title every year. Torre's Yankees were only slightly less successful, winning four world championships

When he took over the Yankees, no one expected Stengel to become a legend. His record of success is irrefutable.

in his first five seasons and making the postseason every year. But unlike Stengel's teams, in order to reach the World Series, Torre's club had to make it through two grueling rounds of playoffs.

Yet Torre, for all his success, probably had the easier task. The Yankees provided him with an almost unlimited budget. Although Torre deserved kudos for creating a team from a collection of stars, his managerial approach didn't stand out.

Casey Stengel, on the other hand, was a true innovator. When he took over the Yankees in 1949, the club was at a crossroads. It was a team of aging stars, including Joe DiMaggio, and a bunch of role players. In order to win, Stengel was forced to improvise. He made great use of the platoon system in his lineup, getting the most out of each player, and he was one of the few managers of his era to recognize the value of the bullpen.

In short, Stengel could take Torre's Yankees and win. Joe Torre might have a hard time doing the same with Stengel's teams.

Joe Torre earned the respect of his players with his quiet, consistent approach. Derek Jeter, for example, referred to him as "Mr. Torre."

Yankee Announcers and the "Voice of God"

Top: Public address announcer Bob Sheppard presents his microphone to the Baseball Hall of Fame in 2000. Sheppard is also in St. John's University Hall of Fame as a first baseman and quarterback in football. *Below:* If Yankee Stadium could speak, it would sound like Sheppard.

Dᴇꜱᴘɪᴛᴇ ᴀʟʟ ᴛʜᴇ ɢʀᴇᴀᴛ players who have called Yankee Stadium home, the most recognizable voice in the ballpark belongs to a modest, unassuming gentleman who once taught high school speech. Born in 1910, Bob Sheppard has been the public address announcer at Yankee Stadium since 1951, earning him the nickname the "Voice of God" for the dignified and unforgettable tone of his voice. When a new player joins the Yankees, he really isn't a member of the team until Sheppard's deep voice introduces him to the masses at Yankee Stadium, where he has been the announcer for some 5,000 games.

Sheppard began his announcing career with the Brooklyn Dodgers football team and joined the Yankees after the Brooklyn team folded. Since then, Sheppard's voice has become as much a part of a game at Yankee Stadium as a Yankee frank. Fans particularly enjoy hearing Sheppard flawlessly enunciate names that most of us find difficult to pronounce, such as Japanese pitcher Shigetoshi Hasegawa or outfielder Raul Ibanez.

Mel Allen's plaque in Monument Park at Yankee Stadium. After retiring as a game broadcaster, Allen hosted the syndicated television program *This Week in Baseball.*

If only that table could talk! From left to right are Phil Rizzuto, Mel Allen, and Red Barber. They are some of the most memorable and distinctive storytellers the game has ever known.

Phil Rizzuto (left) and fellow shortstop Pee Wee Reese (right) both became successful broadcasters after retiring as players.

Several radio and television broadcasters have also been identified with the Yankees over the years. Mel Allen served as the Yankee radio broadcaster from 1939 through 1964. Despite his southern accent (he was from Alabama), New Yorkers loved his soft, comfortable drawl and kids grew up mimicking his signature call, "How about that?"

One of the most beloved Yankee broadcasters was former shortstop Phil Rizzuto. He joined Allen in the broadcast booth in 1957, one year after his retirement as a player, and served as a broadcaster for 40 years. Even though Rizzuto's storytelling sometimes left fans wondering what was happening on the field, they loved his stream-of-consciousness commentary that sometimes mixed a review of his favorite restaurant with a story about a teammate and would end with a force-out at first base, all in the same sentence.

As Rizzuto often said himself, "Holy cow!"

The Greatest Yankees

IT'S NO SECRET. The greatest team in baseball history has often had the greatest players in the history of the game. From Babe Ruth to Derek Jeter, the brightest stars in baseball have often worn pinstripes.

When Joe DiMaggio joined the Yankees in 1936, he was an immediate star. After his rookie season, he was even featured in a Wheaties advertisement.

Left: Although Lou Gehrig and Babe Ruth were not close friends off the field, in the Yankee lineup they combined to create the best power duo in baseball history. *Opposite:* One of the Yankees' greatest strengths has been the way some of the club's greatest players have coexisted on the same team without allowing jealousy or other issues to affect their performance. Although Derek Jeter and Alex Rodriguez are not as close as they were when they became friends early in their careers, they enjoy a successful working relationship.

Babe Ruth

Outfield

Babe Ruth was a member of the inaugural class of five players elected to the Hall of Fame in 1936.

THE GREATEST PLAYER in the history of baseball was a starting pitcher with the Red Sox before being sold to the Yankees following the 1919 season. In New York, Ruth finally found a stage big enough for his talent, becoming a full-time outfielder and the greatest slugger in baseball history.

Ruth changed the game, setting new records by cracking 54 home runs in 1920 and 59 in 1921, turning the also-ran Yankees into an annual pennant contender. He led the Yankees to their first world championship in 1923, and in 1927 his record 60 home runs set the pace for one of the greatest teams in baseball history.

The most beloved Yankee of all time, Ruth led the league in home runs an astounding 12 times. In a famous column, sportswriter John Kieran once posed the question, "Was there ever a guy like Ruth?" More than 70 years since he retired, the answer is still "No." Ruth was one of a kind.

When Yankee owner Jacob Ruppert was on his deathbed in 1939, he asked to see Ruth. When the slugger arrived, Ruppert called him "Babe" for the first and only time.

Ruth's fame transcended the United States. Even at a time when baseball was little known outside North America, Babe Ruth was famous all over the world, which he traveled extensively using this suitcase.

The most familiar photographic image in baseball history may be that of Babe Ruth with a bat in his hand. Every young boy wanted to be Ruth, and emblems such as this one above were designed to be worn on jackets.

Waite Hoyt

Pitcher

WAITE CHARLES HOYT
"SCHOOLBOY"
NEW YORK YANKEE PITCHER 1921-1930.
LIFETIME RECORD: 237 GAMES WON, 182
GAMES LOST, .566 AVERAGE, EARNED RUN
AVERAGE 3.59. PITCHED 3 GAMES IN 1921
WORLD SERIES AND GAVE NO EARNED RUNS
ALSO PITCHED FOR BOSTON, DETROIT AND
PHILADELPHIA A.L. AND BROOKLYN,
NEW YORK AND PITTSBURGH N.L.

Hoyt won 157 games as a Yankee, eighth most in club history. He was elected to the Hall of Fame in 1969.

WAITE HOYT BEGAN his pro career at age 15 with the New York Giants, earning the nickname "Schoolboy." Sent to the minors, he returned to the major leagues with the Red Sox, where he struggled for two seasons before coming to the Yankees in a trade.

The Brooklyn native thrived in New York, winning 19 games in his first season as a Yankee in 1921. Then, in the World Series against the Giants, Hoyt was magnificent in a losing cause, pitching three complete games without giving up an earned run.

Hoyt's greatest seasons came in 1927 and 1928, the only two seasons of his career in which he won 20 or more games. In 1930, he was traded to Detroit, and he retired as a player in 1938.

Hoyt wasn't done with baseball, however. After his retirement, the glib pitcher enjoyed a long career as a broadcaster in New York and Cincinnati. Hoyt was named to the Hall of Fame in 1969.

Although Hoyt went on to pitch effectively for several other teams, he was most effective as a Yankee.

Hoyt is pictured here with the 1927 pitching staff of the Yankees, all of whom have signed the photo on their image. From left to right are Bob Shawkey, Joe Giard, Myles Thomas, Urban Shocker, Waite Hoyt, Herb Pennock, Wilcy Moore, unknown, Dutch Ruether, George Pipgras.

Earle Combs

Outfield

Speedy Earle Combs provided a counterpoint to the power of Ruth and Gehrig, which helped earn him a place in the Hall of Fame. Combs came to the Yankees following a stellar season with minor league Louisville and earned the nickname "The Kentucky Colonel."

NOT EVERY YANKEE STAR has been a power hitter.

Center fielder Earle Combs set the table for Ruth, Gehrig, and other Yankee sluggers. Purchased by the Yankees for $50,000 from Louisville after the 1923 season, Combs was a fixture in the Yankee outfield for the next decade. He was a solid, quiet professional who allowed others to collect the headlines.

Meanwhile, Combs collected hits and runs. Usually batting leadoff, Combs scored more than 100 runs in 8 straight seasons from 1925 through 1932, hitting above .300 in all but one of those years, with a high of .356 in 1927.

In center field he used his great speed to chase down fly balls in Yankee Stadium's vast outfield. That proved to be Combs's only problem: He tried to catch everything. In 1934, he fractured his skull when he collided with the outfield wall. That injury cut short his career.

Combs was named to the Hall of Fame in 1970.

The left-handed hitter was known for his power to the gaps and for his ability to drag bunt for a base hit.

Yankee pitchers appreciated Combs for his ability to run down everything hit his way in center field.

Lou Gehrig

First Base

Had Babe Ruth never existed, Gehrig would probably be considered the greatest power hitter of his time. Gehrig was elected to the Hall of Fame in 1939.

Yankee scout Paul Krichell discovered Gehrig, a native of New York's Upper East Side, playing for Columbia University. When Krichell saw Gehrig hit a long home run that landed on the steps of the Columbia Library, Krichell concluded that he'd found another Babe Ruth. He quickly signed Gehrig to a contract.

After a pinch-hitting appearance on June 1, 1925, Gehrig made the Yankee lineup for good the following day, replacing Wally Pipp, who was forced from the lineup after getting beaned. Gehrig remained in the lineup for the next 2,130 consecutive games, earning the nickname "the Iron Horse."

Gehrig, not Ruth, hit cleanup for the Yankees. Together the two men created the best one-two punch in baseball history. Much more modest and retiring than Ruth, Gehrig was probably the only player who could have survived in Ruth's shadow without shrinking away.

On May 2, 1939, Gehrig removed himself from the Yankee lineup and later learned that he was suffering from amyotrophic lateral sclerosis, now known as Lou Gehrig's disease. He retired with 493 home runs, second at the time to Babe Ruth.

When Gehrig joined Ruth in the Yankee lineup, the Bronx Bombers were born. The two lefty sluggers wore out the right-field bleachers in Yankee Stadium. Gehrig's first baseman's mitt, shown above, saved countless errors from Yankee infielders.

Bill Dickey

Catcher

BILL DICKEY was the consummate catcher. A fine handler of pitchers and possessing a strong arm, Dickey could also hit. Many baseball historians consider him the greatest catcher in baseball history.

A native of Louisiana, Dickey joined the Yankees in 1929. Despite being surrounded by stars such as Ruth and Gehrig, Dickey was not intimidated. He fit right in and hit .324 in his rookie season while providing surprising power.

Playing most of his career under manager Joe McCarthy, Dickey served as a manager on the field, leading sportswriter Dan Daniel to say of him, "He isn't just a player. He's an influence."

Dickey played his entire 17-year career with the Yankees, batting over .300 eleven times, including .362 in 1936, with 202 career home runs.

After he retired as a player, Dickey served as a Yankee coach and was elected to the Hall of Fame in 1954.

Bill Dickey was the second catcher elected to the Hall of Fame by the Baseball Writers' Association of America. For much of his Yankee career, he shared the spotlight with several other Hall of Famers, including Babe Ruth.

Fans may have cheered Babe Ruth, but parents and advertisers, including Post, pointed to Bill Dickey and Lou Gehrig as role models.

Although Dickey was one of the best hitting catchers of his generation, he was also a stalwart defensive player. Many Yankee pitchers improved under his tutelage.

Lefty Gomez

Pitcher

Gomez's 189 victories as a Yankee is third in team history, behind Whitey Ford and Red Ruffing. Gomez twice won the pitching Triple Crown, in 1934 and 1937, helping to guarantee his place in Cooperstown.

THE FUN-LOVING GOMEZ, whom his teammates called "Goofy," joined the Yankees in 1930. He struggled and was sent back to the minors, but in 1931, his fastball and signature leg kick helped him to 21 victories for the Yankees.

Over the next decade, he was one of the most successful pitchers in Yankee history, winning three strikeout crowns, leading the league in ERA twice, and winning more than 20 games four times.

Despite his accomplishments, Gomez never let success go to his head. The self-deprecating pitcher usually gave credit to others, particularly the Yankee outfield, joking that if it were not for the long drives hit off him, Joe DiMaggio never would have become famous for fielding.

Gomez was the winning pitcher in the first All-Star Game in 1933, and in seven World Series starts he was a perfect 6–0.

He was named to the Hall of Fame in 1972.

Gomez signed an orange baseball, which A's owner Chuck Finley tried to introduce in the '70s. The orange baseball never caught on.

Gomez's high leg kick made it tough for hitters to see the baseball, which helped the pitcher lead the American League in strikeouts three times. Of Gomez's contemporaries, only Bob Feller and Lefty Grove were believed to throw harder than Gomez.

Red Ruffing
Pitcher

After failing miserably with Boston, Ruffing joined the Yankees. He experienced one of the greatest turnarounds of any player in the history of the game, forging a Hall of Fame career.

AS A YOUNG MAN, Ruffing worked in a coal mine and lost four toes on his left foot in a mining accident. Despite playing in constant pain, he nevertheless went on to forge a Hall of Fame career.

Ruffing first came to the big leagues with the Boston Red Sox in the 1920s, going a miserable 39–96. Traded to the Yankees during the 1930 season, Ruffing went 15–5 for New York in 1930 and turned his career around.

Tough and durable, Ruffing and Lefty Gomez anchored the Yankee pitching staff during the 1930s. From 1936 through 1939, Ruffing won 20 or more games four seasons in a row. During his career, he was named to six All-Star teams.

He had the full confidence of Yankee manager Joe McCarthy, who usually tabbed Ruffing to start the first game of the World Series. Ruffing rarely disappointed, going 7–2 in ten starts. Ruffing was also one of the best hitting pitchers of all time, hitting .269 for his career with 36 home runs.

When Ruffing became a big winner with the Yankees, his baseball card became a popular collectible.

Ruffing's 261 complete games are the most in club history. In 1932, against Washington, Ruffing threw a shutout and hit a home run in the tenth inning to win the game 1–0. He was the last major-league pitcher to throw a shutout and win the game with a home run in extra innings.

Joe DiMaggio
Outfield

JOSEPH PAUL DI MAGGIO
NEW YORK A.L. 1936 TO 1951
HIT SAFELY IN 56 CONSECUTIVE GAMES
FOR MAJOR LEAGUE RECORD 1941. HIT 2
HOME-RUNS IN ONE INNING 1936. HIT 3
HOME-RUNS IN ONE GAME (3 TIMES). HOLDS
NUMEROUS BATTING RECORDS. PLAYED IN
10 WORLD SERIES (51 GAMES) AND 11 ALL
STAR GAMES. MOST VALUABLE PLAYER
A.L. 1939, 1941, 1947.

Although Joe's brothers Dominic and Vince both played in the major leagues, only Joe DiMaggio earned election to the Hall of Fame.

Long after he retired, DiMaggio is considered by some to be the game's greatest player. His signature is much sought after.

WHILE PLAYING FOR the minor-league San Francisco Seals in 1934, Joe DiMaggio hurt his knee. The injury scared off most clubs, but the Yankees examined DiMaggio and acquired him after the 1935 season for $25,000 and several players.

They never regretted it. DiMaggio stepped into the Yankee lineup in 1936 and was the ultimate professional, leading by example. He was a powerful hitter and center fielder whose graceful defensive play earned him the nickname "the Yankee Clipper" for the way he glided over the outfield.

Over the course of his career, DiMaggio won three MVP Awards, took two batting titles, and led the league in home runs and batting average twice.

In 1941, DiMaggio captured the attention of the nation with a record 56-game hitting streak. Incredibly, as a minor-leaguer in 1933 DiMaggio had hit in 61 consecutive games.

DiMaggio joined the army in 1943 and spent three years in the military before rejoining the Yankees in 1946. He retired after the 1951 season. At the press conference when he announced his retirement, DiMaggio said, "I'd like to thank the good Lord for making me a Yankee."

Here is DiMaggio in 1948 with one of his three MVP Awards.

Yankee fans echoed that sentiment. In his 13 years as a Yankee, DiMaggio led the team to 10 pennants and 9 world championships.

DiMaggio was elected to the Hall of Fame in 1955.

60

DiMaggio was the rare player whose contribution to a team transcended his statistics. He made everyone around him better.

Joe Gordon

Second Base

IN 1938, JOE GORDON struck 25 home runs, a record for a rookie second baseman, and the Yankees had another star. At a time when few middle infielders hit for power, Gordon did. He gave the Yankees a huge advantage.

But Gordon was more than just a good hitter; he could also field. In 1939, he led all AL second basemen in putouts, assists, and double plays. In 1941, he was teamed with rookie shortstop Phil Rizzuto; they were baseball's best double-play combination.

Gordon's best season was 1942. He hit .322 with 103 RBI, leading the Yankees to the pennant and edging out Triple Crown winner Ted Williams of Boston for the MVP Award.

In 1944, Gordon joined the army and spent two seasons in the service before rejoining the Yankees. After a subpar year, he was traded to Cleveland in 1946 and later served as manager for the Indians, Tigers, A's, and Royals.

Left: Joe Gordon is best known for his offense, but his peers knew him as one of the best and most athletic second basemen of his generation. *Below:* Yankee manager Joe McCarthy insisted that every member of his ballclub know how to play the game the right way. Joe Gordon was a complete player. Here he slides home trying to beat the tag.

Young fans enjoyed collecting pennants of Yankee players, including this one of second baseman Joe Gordon, as much as the Yankees enjoyed collecting American League flags.

Phil Rizzuto

Shortstop

Although Rizzuto was surrounded by Hall of Famers such as Yogi Berra and Joe DiMaggio, he won his share of awards—not to mention World Series rings and his own induction into the Baseball Hall of Fame in 1994.

BOTH THE BROOKLYN DODGERS and the New York Giants took one look at the teenage Phil Rizzuto, who stood 5′6″, and told him he was too small to play baseball. But at a 1937 tryout with the Yankees, they saw beyond his stature and signed him to a contract.

After hitting .347 for minor-league Kansas City in 1940, Rizzuto joined the Yankees in 1941. He was a throwback, a player who could bunt for a hit, steal a base, and move runners along the basepaths. The great Ty Cobb believed that Rizzuto was one of the few "modern" players who would have thrived in the dead-ball era.

Rizzuto, nicknamed "Scooter," enjoyed his best season in 1950, hitting .324 and scoring

"Holy Cow!" Rizzuto's signature call was familiar to every Yankee fan from the 1960s to the mid-1990s. Transcripts of Rizzuto's stream-of-consciousness broadcasts were transcribed into free verse and published in a volume of poetry.

125 runs, a performance that earned the shortstop the MVP Award.

After retiring as a player, Rizzuto enjoyed a long career as a Yankee broadcaster. Rizzuto was elected to the Hall of Fame in 1994, his 28th year of eligibility.

Although Rizzuto was not blessed with a strong arm, he got rid of the ball quickly and always seemed to throw out runners by a half-step.

Whitey Ford

Pitcher

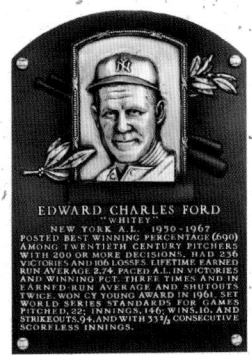

For a franchise known for its sluggers, Whitey Ford may be the greatest pitcher in club history, which earned him a place in the Hall of Fame.

FORD WAS BORN in Manhattan and raised in Queens, but he earned fame in the Bronx. The little left-hander is the greatest starting pitcher in Yankee history and one of the greatest in the history of the game.

Ford was never intimidated. In 1950, as a rookie, he went 9–1 and then won the final game of the World Series. Drafted into the army, Ford—whose light-blond hair earned him the nickname Whitey—rejoined the Yankees in 1953 and immediately became the leader of the staff.

He enjoyed his greatest success after the 1960 season, when Yankee manager Ralph Houk went to a strict four-man pitching rotation, increasing Ford's workload. He won a career-high 25 games in 1961 and added 24 wins in 1963.

In the 1961 World Series, Ford broke Babe Ruth's record of 29⅔ consecutive scoreless innings, a mark Ford eventually raised to 33⅔ innings.

Ford retired in 1967 and was elected to the Hall of Fame in 1974.

Although Ford didn't have an overpowering fastball, he still managed to set the franchise record with 1,956 strikeouts. His success made him a favorite for advertisers.

They called Ford "the Chairman of the Board" for the cool and efficient way he anchored the Yankee pitching staff. His given name is Edward Charles Ford.

Mickey Mantle

Outfield

MICKEY CHARLES MANTLE
NEW YORK A.L. 1951-1968
HIT 536 HOME RUNS. WON LEAGUE HOMER TITLE
AND SLUGGING CROWN FOUR TIMES. MADE
2415 HITS. BATTED .300 OR OVER IN EACH
OF TEN YEARS WITH TOP OF .365 IN 1957.
TOPPED A.L. IN WALKS FIVE YEARS AND
IN RUNS SCORED SIX SEASONS. VOTED
MOST VALUABLE PLAYER 1956-57-62. NAMED
ON 20 A.L. ALL-STAR TEAMS. SET WORLD
SERIES RECORDS FOR HOMERS, 18; RUNS, 42;
RUNS BATTED IN, 40; TOTAL BASES, 123;
AND BASES ON BALLS, 43.

Mickey Mantle and Whitey Ford earned election to the Hall of Fame in 1974.

FEW PLAYERS IN baseball history have been blessed with the combination of speed and power possessed by the young Mickey Mantle. Unfortunately, a number of serious knee injuries eventually stripped Mantle of much of his speed, and his hard living cut his career short. He still put together a remarkable career, but some believe it could have been even better.

Named after Hall of Fame catcher Mickey Cochrane, Mantle joined the Yankees in 1951 and eventually took over for Joe DiMaggio in center field. A switch-hitter, Mantle could beat out a bunt for a hit or knock the ball over the most distant wall for a home run.

In 1956, he won the Triple Crown by batting .353 with 52 home runs and 130 RBI. And, in 1961, he and Roger Maris chased Babe Ruth's home run record for much of the season before injuries knocked Mantle from the lineup late in the year.

Mantle enjoyed his last great season in 1964; he moved over to first base in 1967 before retiring after the 1968 season. He was elected to the Hall of Fame in 1974.

Near right: Mantle was the favorite player of an entire generation of fans, especially kids who wanted to buy products endorsed by Mantle, such as this pencil set.

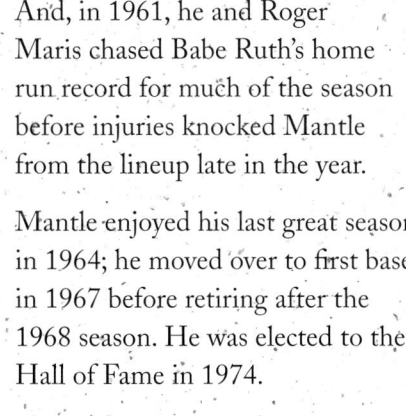

Mantle was a better hitter batting right-handed but displayed greater power when hitting from the left. His father and grandfather taught him to be a switch-hitter.

Yogi Berra

Catcher

Berra grew up in "the Hill" neighborhood in St. Louis along with catcher and broadcaster Joe Garagiola. Berra and Bill Dickey are the only Yankee catchers in the Hall of Fame.

Yogi Berra is perhaps the most unlikely looking player in baseball history. He stood only 5'8" and had a face cut from the funny pages, and then there was his fractured sense of the English language. But on a team of stars, Berra was the one player who was often irreplaceable.

The free-swinging Berra was a natural hitter, but catching didn't come quite so easily. Yet under the tutelage of Bill Dickey, Berra developed into a fine defensive receiver, surprisingly quick and with a strong arm.

A favorite of manager Casey Stengel, Berra was the heart and soul of the Yankees during the 1950s. He won the AL MVP Award three times; no Yankee ever won more.

Following his retirement as a player, Berra served the Yankees in several capacities, including as manager. One of the most beloved Yankees of all time, Berra's malapropos, such as "It's déjà vu all over again," have become part of the American vernacular.

When Yogi Berra first reached the major leagues, he was still known by his given name, Larry, as shown on this baseball card.

Although Berra wasn't speedy, he was quick to react, which made him adept at fielding bunts and slow rollers and chasing down foul pop-ups.

Mel Stottlemyre

Pitcher

IN RECENT YEARS, most Yankee fans know Mel Stottlemyre as the Yankee pitching coach under manager Joe Torre. But during the 1960s, Stottlemyre was one of the best pitchers in baseball. If not for injuries, he may well have earned induction into the Hall of Fame.

The Washington state native was called up by the Yankees midway through the 1964 season. He went 9–3 the rest of the way, then faced Cardinal great Bob Gibson three times in the World Series, going 1–1 with one no decision.

Using a sinking fastball and impeccable control, Stottlemyre anchored the Yankee staff for the next decade, winning 20 or more games in 1965, 1968, and 1969, despite the fact that the Yankees finished below .500 in two of those seasons.

A five-time All-Star, Stottlemyre was forced into retirement after the 1974 season due to injuries. He became the Yankee pitching coach in 1996, survived a bout with cancer, and retired after the 2005 season.

In the dreary late 1960s, one reason for optimism was the fact that every fourth day, Mel Stottlemyre took the mound and throttled the opposition, forcing ground ball after ground ball.

As pitching coach for manager Joe Torre from 1996 through 2005, Stottlemyre helped tutor Mariano Rivera, Chien-Ming Wang, and other Yankee success stories. His sons Todd and Mel, Jr., also pitched in the major leagues.

Graig Nettles

Third Base

GRAIG NETTLES was acquired by the Yankees in a trade with the Cleveland Indians after the 1972 season. For the next decade, he manned third base for the Yankees, earning five trips to the All-Star Game.

Although Nettles did not hit for a high average, he was one of the best power hitters of his era and led the American League with 32 home runs in 1976. In 1977, he hit 37 home runs and knocked in 107 runs, both career highs.

He is best remembered for his performance in the 1978 World Series. After the Yankees fell to the Dodgers in the first two games, Nettles put on a fielding clinic at third base in Game 3, making one spectacular diving grab after another. He saved at least five runs and turned the Series around as the Yankees went on to take four straight games to win the world championship.

Nettles left New York in a trade in 1984 and retired after the 1988 season.

NEW YORK **3rd BASE**

GRAIG NETTLES **YANKEES**

Above: Ever alert on the field, Nettles was known for his diving catches. He was just as quick in the clubhouse, where his ability to cause some mischief and then disappear earned him the nickname "Puff." *Left:* Though he mostly played third base, as stated on his baseball card, on occasion he filled in at shortstop.

Ron Guidry
Pitcher

In 1978, Yankee pitcher Ron Guidry enjoyed perhaps the greatest season of any pitcher in Yankee history. The player they called "Louisiana Lightning" was almost unhittable.

After playing parts of two seasons with the Yankees in 1975 and 1976, Guidry perfected a slider in 1977. He surprised the Yankees by becoming the ace of the staff and winning 16 games.

He was magnificent in 1978. During the first half of the season, as the Red Sox jumped out to an enormous lead, Guidry kept the Yankees in the race almost by himself. On June 17, he set a Yankee record with 18 strikeouts. Then, when the Yankees got hot in the second half, Guidry continued his stellar performance and drew the starting assignment for the one-game playoff versus Boston.

Pitching on only three days rest, Guidry struggled but still managed to win. He finished the season with a record of 25–3, a 1.74 ERA, and 248 strikeouts.

Although Guidry never quite duplicated his 1978 success, he remained an effective pitcher for another decade, winning 21 games in 1983 and 22 in 1985. He retired after the 1988 season and became the Yankee pitching coach in 2006.

Left: Guidry was blessed with one of the best fastballs in the game. When reliever Dick Tidrow helped Guidry learn the slider during spring training in 1977, Guidry blossomed into one of the game's elite pitchers. *Above:* In 2006, Guidry took over for Mel Stottlemyre as Yankee pitching coach. Here he works with Carl Pavano.

Reggie Jackson
Outfield

REGINALD MARTINEZ JACKSON
"MR. OCTOBER"
KANSAS CITY, A.L. 1967
OAKLAND, A.L. 1968-1975, 1987
BALTIMORE, A.L. 1976
NEW YORK, A.L. 1977-1981
CALIFORNIA, A.L. 1982-1986
EXCITING PERFORMER WHO PLAYED FOR 11 DIVISION WINNERS AND
FOUND SPECIAL SUCCESS IN WORLD SERIES SPOTLIGHT WITH 10 HOME
RUNS, 24 RBI'S AND .357 BATTING AVERAGE IN 27 GAMES. IN 1977
SERIES, HIT RECORD 5 HOMERS, 4 OF THEM CONSECUTIVE, INCLUDING
3 IN ONE GAME ON 3 FIRST PITCHES OFF 3 DIFFERENT HURLERS.
MAMMOTH CLOUT MARKED 1971 ALL STAR GAME. 563 HOMERS RANK
6TH ON ALL-TIME LIST. A.L. MVP, 1973.

Although Jackson entered the Hall of Fame as a Yankee, he also starred for the A's, Orioles, and Angels.

Jackson signed this baseball on the sweet spot, but he also hit the sweet spot hard enough to collect 563 career home runs.

SOON AFTER REGGIE JACKSON joined the Yankees, he told a reporter that "I'm the straw that stirs the drink." Jackson was a player whose prodigious talent was matched only by the size of his own ego, and his words immediately got him into trouble with his teammates. Fortunately, when Jackson let his bat do the talking he was usually forgiven.

Jackson gained free agency after the 1976 season, and Yankee owner George Steinbrenner signed him against the wishes of manager Billy Martin. Martin and Jackson immediately clashed, but Jackson played a major role in leading the Yankees to world championships in both 1977 and 1978. Dubbed "Mr. October" by teammate Thurman Munson, Jackson earned the name when he smacked three home runs in Game 6 of the 1977 World Series.

Jackson enjoyed his best season with the Yankees in 1980, hitting .300 with 41 home runs. When his contract expired after the 1981 season, he signed with the California Angels.

After retiring, he rejoined the Yankees, working in a number of capacities. Jackson was elected to the Hall of Fame in 1993.

Reggie Jackson was never more comfortable than in the batter's box, where he was the center of attention.

Willie Randolph

Second Base

I

N THE 1970s AND 1980s, when the Yankees earned the nickname "the Bronx Zoo" due to the histrionics of manager Billy Martin, Reggie Jackson, and others, one player seemed unaffected. Day in and day out second baseman and Brooklyn native Willie Randolph stayed out of the fray. He quietly went about his job, earning everyone's respect.

Acquired from Pittsburgh in exchange for pitcher Doc Medich, Randolph was handed the Yankee second base job in 1976. For the next 13 seasons, while seven different men managed the Yankees, Randolph was the one constant in the Yankee lineup.

Batting second, Randolph was adept at hitting the other way, moving the runner along, and setting the table for the Yankee sluggers behind him. Randolph joined the Dodgers as a free agent in 1989 and later played for the Brewers, A's, and Mets. After serving as a Yankee coach, he moved across town in 2005 and became the manager of the New York Mets.

On a team of big egos, fans appreciated Willie Randolph's steady play and accommodating nature. Randolph often made time to sign baseballs for fans before games.

Left: Randolph, always alert, may well be the best fielding second baseman in club history. *Above:* As coach for the Yankees, Randolph helped middle infielders, including Derek Jeter, adjust to the majors. Here he greets catcher Joe Girardi during the final game of the 1996 World Series.

Goose Gossage
Pitcher

IN THE LATE 1970s AND EARLY 1980s, the most intimidating pitcher in baseball was Yankee reliever Goose Gossage. The hulking pitcher, who stood 6′3″ and sported an unruly Fu Manchu mustache, glared at hitters from the mound and then wound up and dared them to hit his fastball. Few could.

Gossage came to the Yankees as a free agent after the 1977 season, and he took over for popular pitcher Sparky Lyle as the team's relief ace. Gossage, who had been a starting pitcher for the Chicago White Sox in 1976, was a true "fireman" for the Yankees. He didn't just pitch the final inning of a game; he often came in to pitch with men on base in the seventh or eighth inning, put out the "fire," then finished the game.

In both 1978 and 1980, Gossage led the American League in saves, and he saved the 1978 playoff game against Boston, getting Carl Yastrzemski to pop up to end it. In 14 postseason appearances for the Yankees, Gossage won two games and collected seven saves, losing only once.

He left the Yankees after the 1983 season and played another decade before retiring.

Many baseball experts expect that someday Goose Gossage will be able to add the acronym "HOF" to his signed baseballs, representing his election to the National Baseball Hall of Fame, and not just his number as shown above.

Don Mattingly

First Base

No one expected Don Mattingly to become a star. Drafted in the 19th round of the 1979 amateur draft, Mattingly didn't appear big enough to hit for power, didn't run well, and didn't have a strong arm. What he did have was a keen batting eye and a big heart.

After hitting at every level in the minor leagues, Mattingly made his major-league debut in 1982 and hit his way into the Yankee lineup for good in 1984. For most of the next five years he was the best batter in baseball, hitting for a high average, cracking 25 to 30 home runs a season, and driving in runs in bunches. He won the MVP Award in 1985 and earned the respect of every player in baseball with his hard-nosed intensity. Minnesota outfielder Kirby Puckett accurately described him as "Donnie Baseball."

Chronic back trouble affected his production in the 1990s, but during an era in which the Yankees often struggled, Mattingly gave Yankee fans something to cheer about. And when the Yankees finally made the post-season in 1995 for the first time in Mattingly's career, Donnie Baseball didn't disappoint, hitting .417. After sitting out the 1996 season with a sore back, Mattingly retired.

Still as popular today—and as sought after for his autograph—as when he was an active player, Mattingly now serves as Joe Torre's hitting coach with the Dodgers.

During an era in which the Yankees changed middle infielders like T-shirts on a hot day, Mattingly gave the club much needed stability.

Derek Jeter

Shortstop

DEREK JETER WAS BORN to be a Yankee. A native of New Jersey, Jeter moved with his family to Michigan, but he often spent summers in New Jersey with his maternal grandparents. His grandmother's love of the Yankees was transferred to her grandson. Whenever young Jeter was asked what he wanted to do with his life, he said that he wanted to play shortstop for the Yankees.

After a stellar high-school career, Jeter was drafted by the Yankees in the first round of the 1992 draft. In 1996, manager Joe Torre made Jeter his starting shortstop.

Joe Torre became the manager of the Yankees in 1996. In one of his first major decisions, he named rookie Derek Jeter the team's starting shortstop.

Jeter was an immediate star, and the Yankees have made the postseason in every year of his career. A fine fielder, quick runner, and accomplished hitter, Jeter has been named MVP of the World Series and All-Star Game, and he finished second in balloting for the MVP Award in 2006.

The most popular Yankee of his era, Jeter is perhaps best known for his spectacular flip to Jorge Posada to put out Jeremy Giambi during the 2001 playoffs.

Yankee fans have grown accustomed to Jeter's athletic play at shortstop. His arm strength enables him to make a good throw even when airborne.

Bernie Williams

Outfield

YANKEE SCOUTS DISCOVERED Bernie Williams in Puerto Rico while they were scouting future major-leaguer Juan Gonzalez. Williams was a teenage track star, and his speed and long, lean frame reminded the scouts of a young Dave Winfield.

But baseball didn't come naturally to Williams. He slowly worked his way through the minor leagues and didn't join the Yankees for good until his seventh professional season, in 1992.

Over time, Williams learned to harness his speed and athleticism to become a Gold Glove outfielder and one of the most productive hitters in baseball, usually hitting around .300 with 20 or more home runs and 100 RBI.

Williams won the batting title in 1998 with a .339 average, but he really made his mark in the postseason, when he became one of the most productive hitters in baseball history. He earned the ALCS MVP Award in 1996.

A worthy successor in center field to DiMaggio and Mantle, Williams is also an accomplished musician and composer. A jazz guitarist, Williams released a critically acclaimed CD in 2003 entitled *The Journey Within*.

Above: Williams can often be found playing a guitar when he isn't playing ball. *Left:* Williams blossomed from a tentative rookie into one of the most complete players in the game. After the Yankees first scouted Williams, they helped him enroll in a prep school in Connecticut to keep other teams from finding him until he became old enough to sign.

Mariano Rivera

Pitcher

THE KEY TO relief pitcher Mariano Rivera's success is his cut fastball, a pitch that bores in on left-handed hitters and tails away from right-handers. Every hitter knows the pitch is coming, but for more than a decade they have been almost powerless to hit it.

Rivera's pitching career got off to a late start. Until the age of 20, he was a shortstop. Then a Yankee scout saw him pitch, and he was signed to a minor-league contract.

Rivera first made his mark on the Yankees in 1996, serving as a set-up man for closer John Wetteland. When Wetteland left as a free agent in 1997, Rivera took over as closer. Since then he has been nothing short of magnificent, leading the league in saves three times.

Rivera has saved his best work for the postseason. Through the 2008 season, in 76 postseason appearances, Rivera has saved 34 games with a miniscule 0.77 ERA.

When a baseball is in the right hand of Mariano Rivera, no baseball bat is safe. His cut fastball results in dozens of broken bats each season.

For most Yankee fans, the most comforting sight imaginable is Mariano Rivera pitching with a lead in the ninth inning. He credits his great faith for his ability to remain calm in tense situations. Rivera built a church in his native Panama and preaches during the off-season.

Alex Rodriguez

Third Base

After the 2003 season, the Boston Red Sox thought they had a trade in place to acquire Alex Rodriguez from the Texas Rangers, who no longer wanted to pay A-Rod the balance of his $252 million contract, the most lucrative in baseball history. But when financial considerations couldn't be worked out and the Red Sox backed off, the Yankees swooped in and acquired Rodriguez for Alfonso Soriano.

Rodriguez, a Gold Glove shortstop, agreed to move to third base when he joined the Yankees. The leading hitter of his generation and widely considered the best player in the game, Rodriguez struggled in his first season as a Yankee. But he returned to form in 2005, setting a Yankee home run record for right-handed hitters with 48 and winning the MVP Award.

In 2006, however, Rodriguez struggled for much of the year. He discovered that with the game's biggest salary came the game's highest expectations. A-Rod responded in 2008 with a huge year, belting 54 homers, driving in 156 runs, and winning another AL MVP Award. His reputation was tarnished in 2009, however, after he admitted to using steroids.

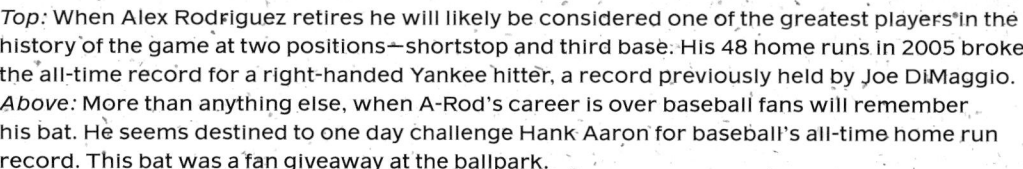

Top: When Alex Rodriguez retires he will likely be considered one of the greatest players in the history of the game at two positions—shortstop and third base. His 48 home runs in 2005 broke the all-time record for a right-handed Yankee hitter, a record previously held by Joe DiMaggio.
Above: More than anything else, when A-Rod's career is over baseball fans will remember his bat. He seems destined to one day challenge Hank Aaron for baseball's all-time home run record. This bat was a fan giveaway at the ballpark.

Mantle or DiMaggio?

IMAGINE FOR A MOMENT that Yankee manager Casey Stengel had the option of choosing between Joe DiMaggio and Mickey Mantle in their prime. Whom would he have chosen?

Beginning in 1936, for more than 30 years, center field in Yankee Stadium was home to either Joe DiMaggio or Mickey Mantle. Yet the careers of the two players overlapped only briefly, in 1951, when DiMaggio, at age 36, was in his last season and Mantle was a 19-year-old rookie. When DiMaggio retired, a torch was passed from one man to the other: Mantle, like DiMaggio before him, took over as the quintessential Yankee of his era, the leader of the team.

As a rookie, each man was ballyhooed as the best prospect of his generation. DiMaggio was an instant star, leading the team to its first pennant since 1932. After only five seasons as a Yankee, his .343 batting average was sixth all time and his 168 home runs were already in the top 20. Then in 1941, before joining the military after the

Mantle not only replaced Joe DiMaggio in the Yankee outfield, but he also became the team's most popular player. Mantle's picture on a magazine cover, like this issue of *Inside Baseball*, guaranteed strong sales.

1942 season, DiMaggio capped off the start of his career with a record 56-game hitting streak, his second MVP Award, and his fifth world championship. Although he wasn't the same player after World War II, DiMaggio still managed to win another MVP Award in 1947.

Mickey Mantle, for all his prowess and natural ability, just doesn't quite compare. DiMaggio arrived in the major leagues ready-made, but it took Mantle several seasons to harness his considerable talent, and almost from the start he was dogged by a series of serious leg injuries that eventually stripped him of much of his speed and athleticism. While Mantle clearly had more raw power than DiMaggio, he was not his equal in the field and Mantle didn't have the immediate impact on the Yankees that DiMaggio did. Besides, as Yankees, the final measurement of a player is world championships. DiMaggio collected 9 in 13 seasons. In 18 seasons, Mantle's Yankees won only 7.

Sorry, Mick, but Casey's picking Joe.

DiMaggio was one of the first Italian-Americans to become a celebrity. The son of immigrants lived the American dream, rising from the San Francisco waterfront to become one of the most recognized people in America, as shown on this magazine cover.

Gossage or Rivera?

WHEN RELIEF PITCHER Rich "Goose" Gossage joined the Yankees as a free agent in 1978, he pushed aside popular closer Sparky Lyle. Although he struggled at the start of the season, Yankee fans soon realized why owner George Steinbrenner had so badly wanted Gossage.

When he took the mound, the hulking Gossage was the most intimidating pitcher in baseball. Blessed with one of the best fastballs in the game, Gossage glared at hitters with contempt and dared the batters to dig in and try to hit him. Few could, and in six seasons as a Yankee, Gossage led the league in saves twice and made four All-Star teams.

In recent years, he has come excruciatingly close to earning election to the National Baseball Hall of Fame, an honor he richly deserves. Unlike the closers of today, Gossage didn't just pitch the final inning of a game. He was a true old-school "fireman," often coming into the game in the sixth or seventh inning with men on base, killing rallies, and then finishing the game off.

Yet for all of Gossage's accomplishments, the greatest reliever in Yankee history, and perhaps the greatest reliever in the history of baseball, is Mariano Rivera. No other relief

The intimidating presence of relief pitcher Goose Gossage signaled the end of the game for many Yankee opponents.

pitcher has been so good, for so long, in so many tough situations as the soft-spoken Panamanian.

Although Rivera is usually called upon to pitch only one inning, whenever manager Joe Torre asked him to do more, as in his three-inning stint in Game 7 of the 2003 ALCS against the Red Sox, Rivera has answered the call.

In fact, it is his performance in the postseason that separates Rivera from the crowd. While Gossage was good in the postseason, going 2–1 with 8 saves in 19 appearances, Rivera has been almost superhuman. On 76 different occasions, the Yankees manager has pointed to his right arm and called for Rivera. He has accumulated an 8–1 record with 34 saves—27 of them working more than one inning—and a miniscule 0.77 ERA in the most tension-filled moments of the most important games his team has played.

Put it this way, if Mariano Rivera were a free agent and joined a team that already had Gossage in the bullpen, at the first sign of trouble Rivera takes the mound. Goose Gossage stays in the pen.

Rivera's extraordinary success stems from a command of a single pitch, a cut fastball that batters find almost impossible to hit.

Yankee Comets

Although the Yankees have had more than their share of stars and superstars, not every Yankee has been an unqualified success. The Yankees have had more than their share of "comets," players who experience early success only to fade away due to injury, bad luck, or other causes.

Perhaps the greatest "comet" in early Yankee history was outfielder Birdie Cree. A near dead ringer for Derek Jeter, Cree made his New York debut in 1908, became a regular in 1910, and after hitting .348 in 1911, was considered the near equal of Ty Cobb and Tris Speaker. Unfortunately, in 1912, a Buck O'Brien pitch broke Cree's arm. He never fully recovered, and after 1915 he was out of baseball.

In more recent years, young sluggers including Joe Lefebvre and Kevin Maas enjoyed moments of early success before fading away, but none had quite the impact of Yankee outfielder Shane Spencer. A journeyman minor-league outfielder, Spencer

As a rookie in 1990, first baseman Kevin Maas set a record with 10 home runs in his first 77 at-bats, finishing with 21 for the season. Unfortunately, he was unable to keep up the pace. He left baseball in 1995 with only 65 career home runs.

After outfielder Birdie Cree's spectacular performance in 1911, he was widely considered one of the greatest players of his era. After injuries ruined his career, Cree became a successful banker.

rode the shuttle between Columbus and New York for much of the 1998 season before being called up for good on August 31.

For the next month he was Babe Ruth, Roger Maris, and Lou Gehrig all wrapped up together, as good as any Yankee hitter has ever been. He hit .421 in September and ended the season with 10 home runs and 27 RBI in only 67 at-bats. Although Spencer

Pitcher Aaron Small bailed out the Yankee pitching staff in 2005 using impeccable pitch selection and command to make up for his lack of speed. For half the season, he was the most successful pitcher in the game.

played six more seasons in the major leagues, he never again approached his early success.

Then there is pitcher Aaron Small, a high school teammate of Jason Giambi and Cory Lidle. After being drafted in 1989, Small bounced around pro baseball for the next 16 years with limited success. He was released five different times before being signed by the Yankees as a free agent in 2005. When injuries decimated the Yankee pitching staff, Small, who was pondering retirement at the time, was called up. He was sensational for the rest of the year, going 10–0 with an ERA of only 3.20. Unfortunately, like these other Cinderellas, the clock soon struck midnight for Small. After starting the 2006 season on the disabled list, Small's ERA ballooned to 8.46 later that year and he was returned to the minors.

Outfielder Shane Spencer was considered only a marginal prospect before his call-up in 1998. He responded with one of the greatest months any Yankee hitter has ever experienced.

Yankee Free Agents

From 1920 through the mid-1960s, the Yankee dynasty was built around scouting and the farm system. Yankee scouts missed few real prospects, and the club had the financial resources to outbid most other teams. As a result, the Yankee farm system supplied the club with an almost unending stream of talent.

By the 1970s, however, that all changed. The amateur draft, adopted in 1965, leveled the playing field. Not until the mid-1970s did the Yankees regain their competitive advantage.

The reason was free agency. No team has been more adept—or more aggressive—at acquiring talent in the free-agent era than the New York Yankees.

After the 1974 season, Oakland hurler Catfish Hunter was declared a free agent following a contract snafu with the A's. Under new owner George Steinbrenner, the Yankees swept in and outbid every other team in baseball for his services.

It immediately paid off as Hunter won 23 games for New York in 1975 and helped make the team a contender. One year later,

pitcher Andy Messersmith successfully challenged baseball's reserve clause, opening the door, with some restrictions, to a new era of baseball history. The best players in the game were soon available to the highest bidder.

Since then, few teams have outbid the Yankees as free agency has delivered stars

New York's signing of Catfish Hunter after the 1974 season ushered in the free-agent era, changing baseball forever.

Above: Former Boston outfielder Johnny Damon is one of the Yankees' more recent free-agent acquisitions. Not only did he fill a void in the Yankee outfield, but his absence hurt the Red Sox. *Left:* Dave Winfield was one of the best free-agent acquisitions in Yankee history. Winfield was a perennial All-Star and earned election to the Hall of Fame.

Likable DH/first baseman Jason Giambi signed a seven-year contract worth $120 million with the Yankees after the 2001 season. Although Giambi hit with power for New York, his batting average was disappointing and he had trouble staying healthy.

Pitcher Mike Mussina has been a success in pinstripes, anchoring the starting rotation since signing as a free agent after the 2000 season.

such as outfielders Reggie Jackson, Dave Winfield, and Johnny Damon; first baseman Jason Giambi; and pitchers Tommy John, Goose Gossage, and Mike Mussina.

Of course, every free agent signed by the Yankees hasn't been a success, as the team also paid big money for disappointments, including outfielder Steve Kemp, pitcher Ed Whitson, and others. But in general, the Yankees have spent their money wisely. Although some have criticized them as "the best team money can buy," the truth is that the Yankees have been most successful when they have used free agency to supplement home-grown stars such as Bernie Williams, Derek Jeter, and Mariano Rivera.

Outfielder Steve Kemp (bottom) collides with teammates while trying to catch a fly ball. Kemp, who was signed by the Yankees as a free agent after the 1982 season, stumbled as a Yankee following an All-Star performance with the Detroit Tigers.

Greatest Fall Classics

It doesn't seem like October unless the Yankees are in the World Series. And with good reason. The Yankees have participated in some of the most memorable World Series in baseball history. With 39 World Series appearances and 26 world championships, the Yankees almost have a permanent reservation to the fall classic.

The Yankees proudly displayed their championship banners on this sketchbook.

Left: In many Octobers there has been no happier place than the Yankee clubhouse after a World Series victory. Here Billy Martin and Mickey Mantle (left to right, top row) and Gil McDougald, Jim McDonald, and Gene Woodling (bottom row) celebrate a win over Brooklyn in Game 5 of the 1953 World Series. *Right:* It takes a team to win a championship. The Yankees stand as one and celebrate their win over the Padres in the 1998 World Series.

1923: Ruth Hot, Giants Not—Yanks Win First Title

IT HAD TO start somewhere. After the New York Giants defeated the Yankees in the World Series in both 1921 and 1922, the Giants expected to win again in 1923. Although Babe Ruth had been dominant in the regular season, thus far the Giants had shut the slugger down in the Series. Without Ruth, the Yankees hadn't found a way to win. Not so in 1923.

After the Giants won Game 1, Ruth came alive in Game 2, smacking two home runs to lead the Yankees to a 4–2 win. At that point, the Giants decided to change strategy.

Determined not to let Ruth beat them, the Giants pitched around Ruth, walking him six times in the next four games. But the Giants soon dis-covered that the Yankees were not a one-man team.

Ruth's teammates picked up the slack. There was a new hero every game as the Yankees out-hit and out-pitched the Giants, winning three of the next four games to win their first world championship.

Opening Day of 1923 was pictured on the cover of sheet music for the song "It's a Grand Old Game." And 1923 was a grand year for the Yankees. They started playing in their new stadium, and they won their first world cham-pionship.

Above: In 1923, Babe Ruth spotted a four-year-old boy playing catch with his father in a park along Riverside Drive. Impressed with the child's ability, Ruth invited little Ray Kelly to become the Yankees mascot. Here they pose before the first game at Yankee Stadium. *Left:* Waite Hoyt won 17 games for the Yankees in 1923, but he was a bust in the World Series. He started Game 1 and lasted only 2⅓ innings, giving up four runs.

Although the Giants had the Yankees in a rundown in this action photo from the 1923 Series, in the end the Yankees had the Giants on the run, winning the championship in six games.

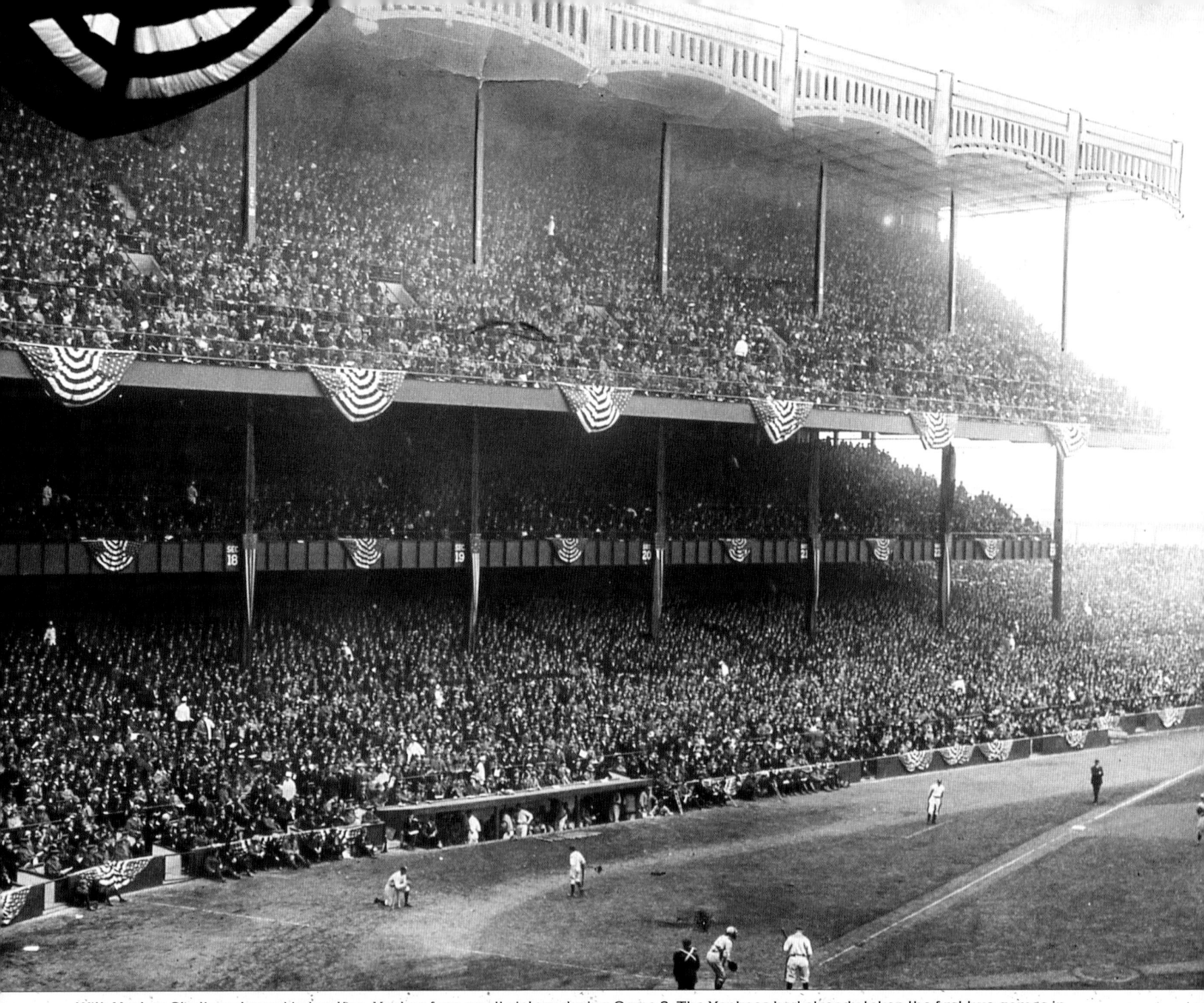

With Yankee Stadium draped in bunting, Yankee fans smell victory during Game 3. The Yankees had already taken the first two games in Pittsburgh, and they captured the world championship with two more victories at home.

1927: Bombers Sweep Pirates

Even contemporary fans continue to celebrate the 1927 world champions, represented by this commemorative patch.

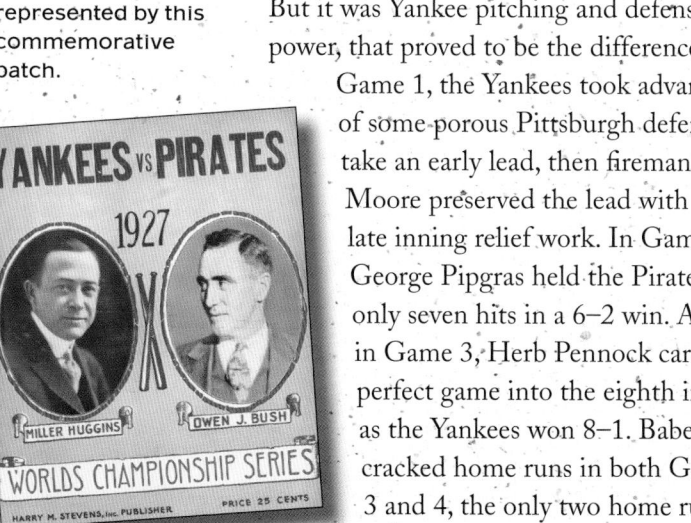

The 1927 World Series matched the strategic acumen of Yankee manager Miller Huggins with his counterpart in Pittsburgh, Pirates manager Owen "Donie" Bush. Both are pictured on this program.

AT A WORKOUT before the start of the 1927 World Series, Babe Ruth looked at the Pittsburgh Pirates, a team that featured three future Hall of Famers in the starting lineup, and told a sportswriter "They look like little kids." When the World Series started, Ruth and the Yankees proceeded to teach the little kids a lesson. As the Yankees swept the Pirates in four games, Pittsburgh led for all of two innings.

But it was Yankee pitching and defense, not power, that proved to be the difference. In Game 1, the Yankees took advantage of some porous Pittsburgh defense to take an early lead, then fireman Wilcy Moore preserved the lead with some late inning relief work. In Game 2, George Pipgras held the Pirates to only seven hits in a 6–2 win. And in Game 3, Herb Pennock carried a perfect game into the eighth inning, as the Yankees won 8–1. Babe Ruth cracked home runs in both Games 3 and 4, the only two home runs the Yankees hit during the Series. Moore, in a rare start, went the distance in the finale, leading to a 4–3 New York win.

Left: Pittsburgh manager Donie Bush and Yankee manager Miller Huggins shared similar backgrounds. Both were former infielders known as terrific fielders and outstanding baserunners. *Below:* Gehrig slid home safely in the third inning of Game 2, scoring on teammate Tony Lazzeri's fly ball to left. The run gave the Yankees a 3–1 lead.

1928: Gehrig, Ruth Blasts Send Cards Home

POOR LOU GEHRIG.

In the 1928 World Series against the St. Louis Cardinals, Gehrig was magnificent. As the Yankees swept the Cards in four straight games, Gehrig belted four home runs, knocked in nine runs, and hit .545 in one of the greatest performances in Series history.

Unfortunately, hardly anyone noticed. That's because Babe Ruth, incredibly, was even better. He hit .625 and cracked three home runs in one game. Together the two sluggers destroyed the Cardinals.

St. Louis manager Bill McKechnie confers with Miller Huggins before the start of the 1928 World Series. A few days later, he would offer Huggins congratulations as the Yankees took the Series.

In the first inning of Game 1, Ruth and Gehrig smashed back-to-back doubles to give the Yankees a 1–0 lead. Ruth's fourth inning double started another rally as the Yankees won 4–1. In Game 2, Gehrig's three-run first inning blast keyed a 9–3 Yankee victory, and in Game 3 Gehrig's two home runs in his first two at-bats led the Yankees to a 7–3 come-from-behind win.

Then came Game 4. Ruth homered in the fourth inning to give the Yankees their first run, and then he homered again in the seventh to tie the game. Gehrig followed with his fourth home run of the Series to put the Yankees ahead 3–2, but Ruth wasn't finished. In the eighth inning, he hit his third home run of the game, capping off a 7–3 victory as the Yankees won their second consecutive World Series.

Left: The Yankees treated the base-paths like a merry-go-round, cracking nine home runs in four games, including a blast by Bob Meusel, who nearly caught up to Babe Ruth as he trotted home.

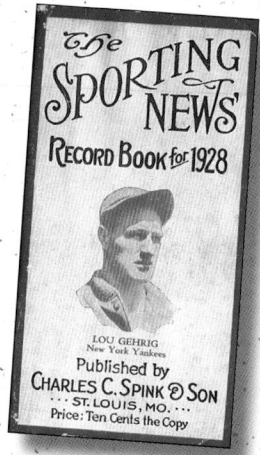

Gehrig's exploits earned him the cover of *The Sporting News Record Book for 1928.*

Even enormous Yankee Stadium seemed too small for the potent Bronx Bombers. The Yanks cracked two home runs at home then added seven more in St. Louis as they swept the Cardinals.

Cub fans grew tired of watching Yankees greet Ruth at home plate; here Gehrig shakes hands with him. The Babe scored six runs during the Series.

1932: Ruth and Gehrig Take Out the Cubs

BABE RUTH'S FAMOUS "called shot" provided the signature moment of the 1932 World Series, but in reality it played a small role in the Yankees' world championship. Inspired by the fact that the Cubs voted shortstop and former Yankee Mark Koenig only a partial share of World Series money, the Yankees soon expressed their displeasure. They thumped the Cubs in four straight games.

Instead of rings, championship teams once distributed other items to players, including medallions, not unlike this contemporary version recalling the 1932 champions.

They did it with power. Lou Gehrig led the charge by keying a Yankee comeback in Game 1 with a two-run home run as New York won 12–6. The Yankees won Game 2 by a score of 5–2.

In Game 3, Ruth cracked a three-run home run in the first inning to put the Yankees ahead. Gehrig then hit a solo home run in the third inning. Ruth's called shot came in the fifth inning off Cubs pitcher Charlie Root and it broke a 4–4 tie. Then Gehrig followed with his second home run of the game.

In Game 4, the Yankees stormed back from a 4–1 first-inning deficit behind two home runs by second baseman Tony Lazzeri to take the game 13–6 and sweep the Cubs.

Above: Ruth's mythic called shot is rendered by artist Robert Thom in this painting entitled "The Mighty Babe." *Left:* Radio broadcaster Ted Husing calls the action of the 1932 World Series from the front row of the upper deck at Yankee Stadium.

1947: Dodgers Left Waiting Again

THE BROOKLYN DODGERS, featuring rookie first baseman Jackie Robinson, the first African American in the major leagues, gave the Yankees all they could handle but fell just short in 1947, losing to New York in seven games. Most fans, however, remember a game the Yankees lost.

Entering Game 4, the Yankees led the Series two games to one. They sent journeyman pitcher Bill Bevens to the mound. Through eight innings, despite giving up eight walks, he nursed a 2–1 lead. Bevens hadn't given up a hit, and in the bottom of the ninth inning he needed only three outs to pitch the first no-hitter in Series history.

It was not to be. Bevens walked two more Dodgers and then pinch hitter Cookie Lavagetto doubled to right field to break up the no-hitter, knock in two runs, win the game for Brooklyn, and tie the Series.

Unfortunately for the Dodgers, they still needed to win two more games. The Yankees came back to win Game 5, and in Game 7 Bevens got another chance. Pitching in relief, he stopped a Brooklyn rally and the Yankees took the game 5–2 to win the Series.

Crowds at both Yankee Stadium and Brooklyn's Ebbets Field were standing room only during the 1947 World Series. Attendance at Game 1 in Yankee Stadium set a new record with 73,365 fans. That's a lot of fans to sell scorecards to.

Good defense has always been a Yankee trademark. Shortstop Phil Rizzuto tries to put the tag on Brooklyn's Al Gionfriddo.

Joe DiMaggio (left) and Joe Page (center) were two of the Yankee big guns in the Series. DiMaggio homered twice and Page pitched 13 innings in relief. Their performances made team president Larry MacPhail (right) a happy man.

Jubilant Yankee fans storm the field at Yankee Stadium after a game in the 1947 World Series against the Dodgers.

Tommy Henrich's ninth-inning, game-winning home run off Don Newcombe in Game 1 gave the Yankees a 1–0 win and sparked a celebration at Yankee Stadium. The crowd loiters on the field after the celebration.

1949: Page Closes Book on Brooklyn

Right: The Yankees' first Series title under manager Casey Stengel was a team victory. Stengel is holding a game ball.

Below: Yankee outfielder Gene Woodling slides home safely past Brooklyn catcher Roy Campanella. Woodling hit .400 in the Series.

WITH JOE DIMAGGIO still recovering from a bout of pneumonia, the Brooklyn Dodgers were heavily favored to win the 1949 Series. The Yankees, however, thought differently. New York manager Casey Stengel, in his first season as Yankee skipper, proved up to the task. He went with the hot hand and the result was another world championship for the Yankees.

In Game 1, pitcher Allie Reynolds shut out Brooklyn 1–0, but in Game 2, Dodger Preacher Roe returned the favor, shutting out the Yankees by the same score. Then Yankee relief pitcher Joe Page and Reynolds took over.

In the wake of World War II, the patriotic Yankee top hat became a familiar symbol for the team, as shown on this patch for the 1949 club.

Page got the win in Game 3 with 5⅔ innings of relief, and Reynolds picked up a save in Game 4. In Game 5, Stengel turned to Page again. He saved the game, and New York won the Series, despite hitting just .226 and smacking only two home runs.

1953: Stengel, Yankees Make It Five

The Yankees began the 1953 World Series in search of a record fifth consecutive world championship. The Dodgers, winners of 105 games that season, stood in their way.

At first the Yankees hardly blinked. In Game 1 they exploded for four first-inning runs and raced to a 9–5 win, then they put Brooklyn on the ropes with a 4–2 win in Game 2. But the Dodgers didn't give in. They knotted the Series by winning Games 3 and 4.

Then the Yankees got serious. Gene Woodling led off Game 5 with a home run, the first of four Yankee home runs that day, and the Dodgers fell 11–7. Five proved to be a lucky number for the Yankees.

In the bottom of the ninth in Game 6, the score was tied 3–3 before a walk to Hank Bauer and an infield hit by Mickey Mantle put the winning run in scoring position. When second baseman Billy Martin followed with a single to center field—his 12th hit of the Series—the Yankees celebrated a record fifth consecutive world championship.

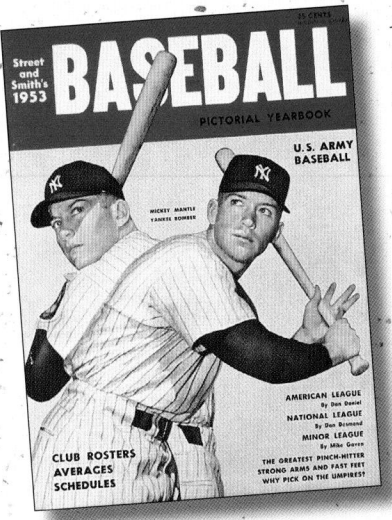

Mickey Mantle's heroics on the field made him a favorite cover figure for many baseball magazines, including the one above.

Above: Both Billy Martin (left) and Mickey Mantle (right) hit home runs in Game 2 to help pitcher Eddie Lopat (center) earn the victory. *Left:* Yankee manager Casey Stengel holds up six fingers to indicate that the Yankees' next goal—after they defeat the Dodgers in the 1953 World Series—is six straight world championships.

CROSETTI

GORE

ROBINSON

SNIDER

REESE

HURLEY

COX

GILLIAM

MANTLE

BAUER

ERSKINE

MARTIN

WOODLING

CAMPANELLA

RIEVE

DICKEY

This labeled photograph shows where Billy Martin's hit dropped between Jackie Robinson and Duke Snider for a single, which scored Hank Bauer and won the Yankees their fifth straight World Series championship.

Pitcher Johnny Kucks is mobbed by teammates after pitching the Yankees to victory in Game 7.

1956: Perfect Game, Perfect Ending

AFTER LOSING TO the DODGERS in the 1955 World Series, the Yankees looked forward to a rematch in 1956. But after the Yankees lost Game 1 and pitcher Don Larsen failed to hold a 6–0 lead in Game 2, which the Yankees lost 13–8, the Dodgers looked like the only team with anything to look forward to.

Fortunately, a rainout after Game 1 gave pitcher Whitey Ford an extra day of rest. He came back to win Game 3, and Tom Sturdivant pitched the Yankees to victory in Game 4, tying the Series. Then came one of the greatest games in the history of the World Series.

In Game 5, Don Larsen was flawless, retiring all 27 Dodgers for the first perfect game in Series history, winning 2–0. Although Brooklyn bounced back to win Game 6 with a score of 1–0, in Game 7 the Yankee offense finally showed up. They pounded four home runs, including two by Yogi Berra, to win 9–0 and take the Series.

A vendor hawks programs during a game, but all eyes are on the action on the field.

The Yankees and Dodgers met in 1956. Pictured is a program for that Series. The 1956 World Series marked the end of an era when every Series seemed to take place in New York.

With the game scoreless, Pee Wee Reese pops up to Yogi Berra in the sixth inning of Game 6. The Dodgers won in the tenth inning, 1–0, forcing Game 7.

1960: Crushed Bucs Walk Off with Win

IN THE 1960 WORLD SERIES, the Yankees did everything but win.

In their three victories, New York humiliated the Pittsburgh Pirates, beating them 16–3, 10–0, and 12–0. But the Yankees also lost 6–4, 3–2, and 5–2, and after six games the Series was tied.

Game 7 was a classic. The Pirates jumped out to a 4–0 lead before the Yankees stormed back behind home runs by Moose Skowron and Yogi Berra to take a 7–4 lead into the eighth inning. Then the Pirates mounted a comeback, scoring five times to go ahead 9–7. The Yankees scored twice more in the top of the ninth inning to tie the game.

In the bottom of the ninth, manager Casey Stengel called on Game 4 losing pitcher Ralph Terry to set down the Pirates. Light-hitting second baseman Bill Mazeroski led off the inning and took the first pitch for a ball. He swung at the next pitch, and it sailed over Yankee outfielder Yogi Berra's head and over the left-field wall at Forbes Field to give the Pirates a 10–9 win and an improbable world championship. Despite outscoring Pittsburgh 55–27, the Yankees lost the Series.

Pirate pitcher Harvey Haddix and Yankee starter Art Ditmar greet each other before taking the mound for Game 5. Haddix earned the win as Ditmar failed to make it through the second inning in New York's 5–2 loss.

Above: The Yankees didn't always win. A dejected Casey Stengel walks off the field and the Pirates celebrate as Bill Mazeroski crosses the plate with his game-ending, Series-winning home run. *Right:* In their three victories, the Yankees treated Pittsburgh pitching like it was batting practice.

Mickey Mantle led the Yankee assault with three home runs during the Series.

Catcher Elston Howard catches pitcher Ralph Terry as he jumps for joy after winning Game 7. Bobby Richardson (hatless) had just grabbed Willie McCovey's line drive to end the game.

1962: Richardson Snags Drive, Series

SOMETIMES IT ALL comes down to one game—and one play.

In the 1962 World Series, the Yankees and San Francisco Giants were evenly matched. Neither team was capable of taking command. The Yankees won Games 1, 3, and 5, while the Giants took Games 2, 4, and 6, setting up a dramatic Game 7.

Both Yankee starting pitcher Ralph Terry and Giant Billy Pierce were at the top of their games. The Yankees scored a single run in the fifth on two singles, a walk, and a double play, but the Giants couldn't touch Terry. Entering the bottom of the ninth, he'd given up only two hits.

But Matty Alou led off the inning by beating out a bunt, and then, with two outs, Willie Mays doubled to put the tying and winning runs in scoring position.

Slugger Willie McCovey, one of the strongest hitters in baseball, hit the ball squarely and sent a rocket toward right field. Fortunately for the Yankees, it went straight into the glove of Yankee second baseman Bobby Richardson. Had the ball been hit a foot or two in either direction, the Giants would have won.

Yankee third baseman Clete Boyer was best known for his fielding prowess, but in the 1962 Series he hit .318 while making two rare errors.

The two best center fielders in baseball squared off in the 1962 Series. Neither man played particularly well, however, as Mantle (left) hit only .120 and Mays (right) batted .250.

Bad weather caused the seven-game Series to be played over a 12-day period. Whitey Ford started three games for the Yankees, including Games 4 and 6, which were played a week apart. Ford won one, lost one, and earned a no-decision.

1977: Reggie, Reggie, Reggie!

AFTER LOSING TO the Reds in the 1976 World Series, the Yankees, who hadn't won a world championship since 1962, were anxious to add another crown.

They won three of the first four games of the Series before the Dodgers rallied to win Game 5, sending the Series back to New York. With one more victory the Yankees would be world champions.

After a quiet playoff series, Yankee outfielder Reggie Jackson, following a tumultuous first season in New York, was having a very good World Series, hitting a home run in both Game 4 and in his last at-bat in Game 5. But everyone remembers Game 6.

After the Dodgers took a 3–2 lead, Jackson came up in the fourth inning and cracked a two-run home run to give the Yankees a 4–3 lead. In the fifth inning, he came up again and hit another two-run home run and the Yankees led 7-3. And when Jackson came to bat in the eighth inning, with every fan in Yankee Stadium calling his name, Reggie put the game away with his third consecutive home run, making the Yankees world champions once again.

Although Catfish Hunter won 23 games while with the Yankees in 1975, arm trouble in 1977 limited him to only nine wins. He struggled in the Series, losing his only start in Game 2.

Gritty outfielder Lou Piniella epitomized the determination of the Yankees.

The goal every spring is to win the World Series trophy in October. Yankee fans whetted their appetite with a photo of the trophy on the World Series program in 1977.

A medallion is one way for fans to commemorate the club's back-to-back world championships in 1977 and 1978.

Dodger fans thought they were stuck in a time warp during Game 6 as Reggie Jackson hit a home run on the first pitch in each of three consecutive at-bats. Here he hits home run number three.

All eyes are on Yankee Stadium as the players are introduced before the start of the 1996 World Series.

1996: Torre Goes to Town

AFTER THE YANKEES lost the first two games of the Series to the Braves, there was already speculation that Joe Torre would be fired. Torre, however, remained confident. After losing Game 1, the former Braves manager told George Steinbrenner that the Yankees would probably lose Game 2 as well, then he added, "Atlanta's my town. We'll take three games there and win it back home."

That's exactly what happened. Before Game 3, Torre juggled the lineup and David Cone pitched the Yankees to a 5–2 win. Then, in Game 4, the Yankees stormed back from a 6–0 deficit before Jim Leyritz tied the game with an eighth-inning home run off Atlanta reliever Mark Wohlers. Then the Yankees won in extra innings.

The Series was tied, but it was over. Andy Pettitte and John Wetteland combined to shut out the Braves 1–0 in Game 5. Just as Torre predicted, the Yankees won it in New York. When third baseman Charlie Hayes caught a pop-up for the final out in Game 6, the Yankees captured their first world championship since 1978.

The Yankees leave the field after their hard-earned victory over the Braves. Over the next four seasons, they would win the Series three more times.

Left: Yankee outfielder Darryl Strawberry hoists the world championship trophy after New York defeated Atlanta. Strawberry resurrected his career with the Yankees in 1996, hitting 11 home runs in part-time duty.

Left: Yankee fans can start each day with a coffee mug emblazoned with the 1996 world championship victory. *Above:* New York City celebrated the Yankees' World Series win by giving the team a ticker-tape parade down the Canyon of Heroes in lower Manhattan.

1998: Yanks Pacify Padres

H O-HUM.

After winning 114 regular-season games, the Yankees stormed through the playoffs, losing only twice before facing the San Diego Padres in the World Series. Brimming with confidence, pitcher David Wells told radio host Howard Stern that the Yankees would beat the Padres in five games before adding, "I'd like to wrap it up in four."

Wells, who went 18–4 in 1998, proved just as adept in making predictions. The Yankees toyed with the Padres.

New York gave San Diego one chance, in Game 1, as the Padres, angry at Wells, knocked him around to take a 5–2 lead. Then the Yankees took command, scoring seven runs to win the game and put the Padres on their heels.

Over the next three games, the Padres held the lead for only one inning. In Game 2, New York won 9–3. In Game 3, the Yankees won 5–4, and Scott Brosius hit two home runs. In Game 4, the Yanks won 3–0 as Andy Pettitte and the bullpen combined for a shutout.

Pitcher David Wells was the beneficiary of Tino Martinez's grand slam in Game 1. Wells was the winning pitcher in that game despite giving up five runs, including back-to-back home runs to Tony Gwynn and Greg Vaughn in the fifth inning.

Scott Brosius celebrates one of his two home runs in Game 3. Brosius drove in four runs, including the game-winner, in New York's come-from-behind 5–4 win.

First baseman Tino Martinez put the Yankees ahead in Game 1 with a grand slam off pitcher Mark Langston. Martinez's seventh-inning blast broke a 5–5 tie and helped the Yankees to a 9–6 win.

Above: This ticket for Game 7 of the 1998 World Series is known as a "phantom." The Series ended in four games, and this ticket was never used. *Left:* The Yankees clinched yet another world championship as Andy Pettitte, Jeff Nelson, and Mariano Rivera combined for a 3–0 shutout to conclude the Yankees' four-game sweep of the Padres.

Members of the New York City Fire Department unfurled the American flag before Game 5 of the 2001 World Series versus Arizona. A flag recovered from the World Trade Center flew over Yankee Stadium during the Series.

2001: Ecstasy and Agony Amid Heartbreak

ONLY THE New York Yankees could lose a World Series and still have it considered one of the most memorable in history.

In the wake of 9/11, the Yankees seemed emotionally and physically exhausted at the start of the Series. The Arizona Diamondbacks, behind pitchers Curt Schilling and Randy Johnson, dominated the Yankees to take the first two games of the Series in Arizona. But when the Yankees returned to New York, the Series turned.

Before a crowd that included President Bush and with a tattered flag recovered from the World Trade Center flying from the center-field flagpole, Roger Clemens got the Yankees back in the Series with a gutsy performance in Game 3. Then, in Game 4, the magic started to happen as the Yankees staged two of the more improbable comebacks in World Series history.

One out away from defeat, Tino Martinez tied the game with a home run, sending the game into extra innings. Then Derek Jeter hit a tenth-inning homer to win the game. The next night, Scott Brosius delivered the Yankees from the brink with a ninth-inning, two-out, game-tying home run. Once again the Yankees won in extra innings.

Unfortunately, the Yankees exhausted their quota of comebacks. The Diamondbacks won Game 6 big, then tallied a comeback of their own in Game 7 to win the Series.

Derek Jeter wears a New York Fire Department (FDNY) hat to honor them. After 9/11, Port Authority Police (PAPD) hats were also popular.

Left: With the opportunity to win the Series, the Yankees were blown out in Game 6. Jorge Posada, Derek Jeter, coach Don Zimmer, and manager Joe Torre look on in disbelief.

After the terrorist attacks on the World Trade Center on September 11, 2001, a Yankee baseball cap symbolized not just the New York Yankees but New York City as well.

The Yankees and Bernie Williams ran out of magic in Game 7 of the Series against the Diamondbacks.

Worst Loss to Boston: The Final Day of the 1904 Season or Game 7 of the 2004 ALCS?

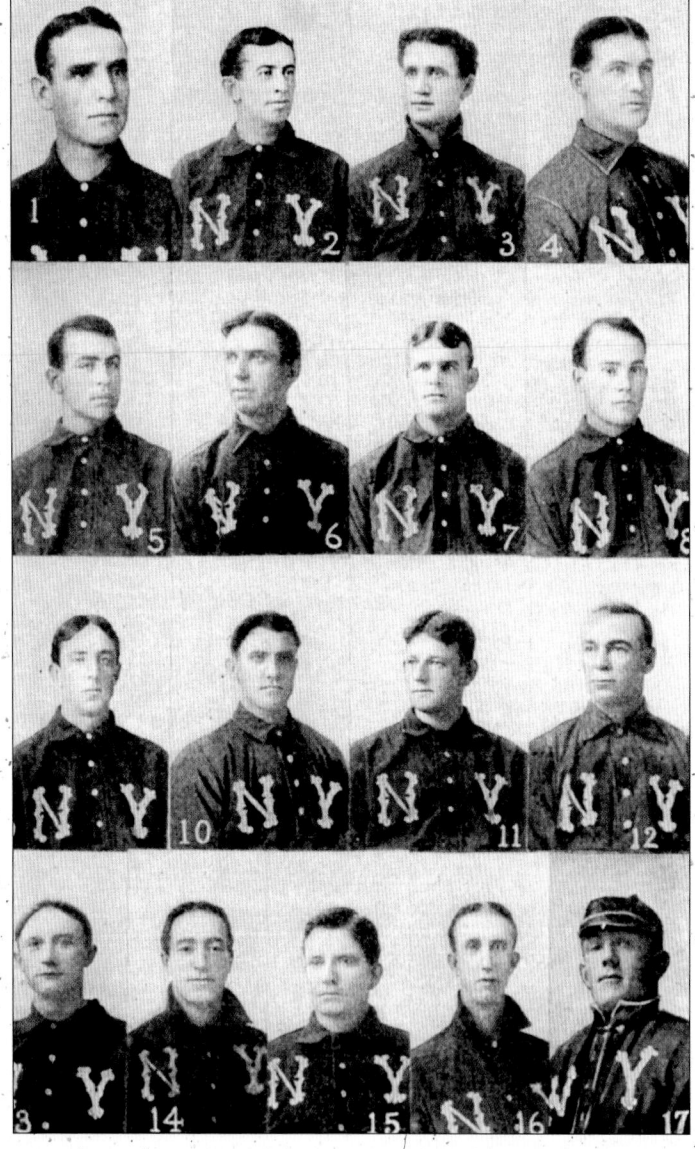

Today's Yankee uniforms may be different, but the passion remains the same as when New York met Boston on the final day of the 1904 season. Pitcher Jack Chesbro (second from right, third row from top) was disconsolate after throwing the wild pitch that decided the game.

Trying to decide whether the Yankees' worst loss to the Boston Red Sox was on the final day of the 1904 season or, 100 years later, their collapse in the 2004 ALCS is like choosing to have either a tooth or a toenail extracted without anesthetic. Both hurt badly.

Contemporary fans would undoubtedly choose the 2004 playoffs as the more painful of the two choices; the Yankees suffered a defeat unlike any other in the history of the game. No other team has ever lost a seven-game series after leading three games to none, and the experience of losing the next four games took place over days, an extended period of suffering unique in the annals of the sport. But by Game 7, most Yankee fans already knew it was over.

Despite the agony of that defeat, however, contemporary fans can fall back on the knowledge that for a full century before 2004, the Yankees beat the Red Sox every single time it mattered. And there are those 26 world championships to make the pain go away.

There was no such solace for Yankee fans in 1904. When the Yankees and Boston met on the final day of the season, more than a pennant was at stake. The NL champion New

York Giants had already announced they would not play the winner of the AL pennant in "world's series" as it was then called. That meant that the winner of the contest between New York and Boston would lay claim to the world championship, the only time in modern baseball history that question has been decided on the final day of the regular season. The Yankees had the more difficult task. Boston needed to win only aa single contest to lay claim to the championship, while the Yankees needed to win both games of the season-ending doubleheader.

Here is how it ended and here is how badly it hurt: Nursing a one-run lead entering the ninth inning of the first game, Yankee pitcher Jack Chesbro, in search of his 42nd victory of the year, uncorked a wild pitch. That single pitch cost his team the game, the pennant, and the world championship. It was the most costly single pitch in the history of baseball. As Chesbro said later, "In all New York I don't believe there was a more sorrowful individual. I would have given my entire year's salary back could I but had the ball back."

Now *that's* pain. The 2004 Yankees were hurt by their loss, but no one offered to give back his salary.

Above: After winning the first three games of the 2004 ALCS, the Yankees lost four games in a row, looking more and more stunned after each defeat. *Left:* The Yankee collapse in the 2004 playoffs against Boston was total and complete. The hitters stopped hitting, and the pitchers couldn't stop the Red Sox. Here Torre pulls Javier Vazquez in Game 7 after he gave up two home runs.

The Skippers

THE YANKEES HAVE HAD more than their share of star players, but without the leadership of managers who earned the respect of those stars, there is no way the Yankees ever would have been as successful.

Miller Huggins was hired in 1918 and became the first great Yankee manager. As a player during the dead-ball era, the second baseman earned a reputation as a heady player. After he retired, he earned a law degree and managed the St. Louis Cardinals before taking over the Yankees.

Huggins stood only 5'4". Despite his small stature, he commanded respect. When Babe Ruth joined the team, Huggins instantly realized that Ruth's power changed the game, and he built his team around Ruth and the home run. More significantly, however, was that over time Huggins was able to rein in the undisciplined Ruth, acting as a father figure for the wayward slugger. After leading the Yankees to three world

Casey Stengel was, in a sense, the perfect Yankee manager. His teams usually won, and when they didn't, Stengel kept Yankee fans smiling.

titles, Huggins passed away during the 1929 season, leaving Ruth and his teammates heartbroken.

The next great Yankee manager was Joe McCarthy, who took over in 1931 after a successful stint with the Cubs. "Marse Joe" expected his players to know how to play the game and to act as professionals. He instituted a businesslike atmosphere on the team. He banned card playing in the clubhouse and insisted that when they were on the road, each player had to wear a suit in public. McCarthy summed up his philosophy in his *Ten Commandments of Baseball*, which included "Do not quit" and "Always run them out. You can never tell." A player who did not adhere to McCarthy's rules did not remain a Yankee for long. His club won eight pennants and seven World Series before McCarthy resigned in 1946.

Casey Stengel became the Yankee manager in 1949. Although Stengel had never won a

Miller Huggins's greatest achievement may have been his ability to keep Babe Ruth in line and focused on baseball. Huggins is pictured here with owner Jacob Ruppert.

Joe McCarthy (right), pictured with Lou Gehrig (left) and sporting goods manufacturer John Hillerich, began many customs that have become part of Yankee tradition.

pennant as manager of the Braves or Dodgers, but he won a pennant in 1948 as manager of minor-league Oakland. That earned him a shot with the Yankees. Although Stengel sometimes acted as if he didn't take the game seriously, he had been a fine player and had learned the game from New York Giants legendary manager John McGraw. Stengel got the most out of his team, winning pennants and world championships in each of his first five seasons.

After Stengel left the Yankees following the 1960 season, the Yankees won two more world championships under Ralph Houk before falling on hard times. The team didn't win another championship until George Steinbrenner hired former Yankee infielder Billy Martin during the 1975 season.

Yankee fans loved manager Billy Martin for his feisty and sometimes combative style.

A protégé and favorite of Casey Stengel, the volatile Martin fought to win every game, even if that meant fighting his own players. Perhaps the best game-situation manager in Yankee history, Martin's players played hard for him, even when they hated him. Under Martin, the team won back-to-back pennants in 1976 and in 1977, when they also won the World Series.

Unfortunately, Martin had a significant drinking problem and quickly wore out his welcome, clashing with players including Reggie Jackson and owner George Steinbrenner. Steinbrenner, however, loved Martin, hiring and firing him no less than five times from 1975 to 1988 before Martin died in a car accident in 1989.

Joe Torre was hired in 1996. It had been 18 years since the Yankees had won a world championship. Although Torre had some success as manager of the Braves and Mets, since being fired as manager of the Cardinals in 1995 Torre had been working as a broadcaster.

Yankee PR advisor Arthur Richman recommended Torre to Steinbrenner. Although at first glance the move seemed curious, Torre had grown up in New York and wasn't intimidated by taking over the Yankees. He made Steinbrenner look like a genius, leading the Yankees to 4 world championships and 12 consecutive postseason appearances. He led the Yankees into their second century of excellence.

Joe Torre earned his way into any discussion of great Yankee managers. He led the Yankees into the postseason for 12 consecutive seasons.

Money, Money, Money

MONEY ISN'T *everything*.

Although in recent years, the Yankees have spent more money on player salaries than any other team in baseball, that hasn't always been the case. In fact, at times the Yankees have been considered the cheapest team in the league.

Their first owners, Frank Farrell and William Devery, were notorious gamblers. Farrell and Devery used the Yankee bank account to finance their addiction, often shortchanging their own players and even selling them off to line their own pockets.

Yankee co-owner Frank Farrell was more concerned with his own bank account than the win-loss record of the Yankees. After selling the team to Jacob Ruppert, Farrell and co-owner William Devery both squandered their fortunes and died almost penniless.

Conditions improved under Yankee owner Jacob Ruppert, who made Babe Ruth the highest paid player in baseball and handsomely rewarded Lou Gehrig. Ruth's salary peaked at $80,000 a year in 1930, while Gehrig earned as much as $39,000 a season.

But the Yankees weren't as generous as other teams. From 1934 through the 1950s, the Boston Red Sox consistently had the highest payroll in baseball. Even Joe DiMaggio had to threaten to hold out to get a decent salary from the Yankees.

In fact, when George Weiss served as general manager from 1947 through 1960 the Yankees were considered cheapskates. Weiss received a percentage of any money left in the budget after he negotiated a player's contract. As a result, when Weiss went into negotiations with Yankee players he argued that the World Series check was part of each players' annual salary, thereby increasing his own take.

Although during the free-agent era the Yankees gained a reputation for free-spending, a number of players have taken less money in

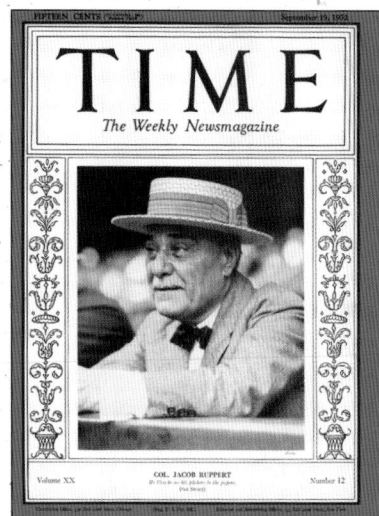

Yankee owner Jacob Ruppert made a fortune with the Ruppert Brewery before buying the Yankees. He treated his players well, particularly at contract time. Here he's pictured on the cover of *Time* magazine.

At the end of the day, the Yankees have always managed to reach an agreement with their greatest players, such as Joe DiMaggio, here pictured with Jacob Ruppert (right).

order to play for the Yankees and have a chance at winning a world championship. When Reggie Jackson signed as a free agent for only $2.5 million over five years in 1976, he turned down a $4 million offer from the Montreal Expos. And although Alex Rodriguez's annual salary of $25 million is the highest in the game, the Texas Rangers are responsible for nearly 40 percent of that amount, making A-Rod a relative bargain.

Even though the Yankees have since spent millions and millions of dollars on players, they have gotten a return on their investment. With 26 world championships, the Yankees have spent less money per world championship than any other team in baseball.

Isn't that the goal?

Above: Yankee general manager George Weiss was a penny-pincher who fought Yankee players over every dime of their contracts. *Left:* When the Yankees traded for Alex Rodriguez in 2004, they acquired baseball's highest paid player, an honor previously held by Yankees such as Babe Ruth, Joe DiMaggio, Mickey Mantle, and Catfish Hunter.

Magical Moments

THE HISTORY OF the New York Yankees is richer than that of any other team in the game. Time and time again, the Yankees have provided their fans with scenes and episodes that are etched in their memories forever. When fans think about the Yankees, these are some of the moments they remember best.

Great Yankee players appear to compete for space on this 1985 yearbook. Each of these players is also responsible for some of the greatest moments in Yankee franchise history.

Left: The home run has long been a Yankee trademark and is responsible for some unforgettable moments. It is impossible to look at a photograph of Roger Maris swinging a bat and not recall his record-setting performance in 1961. *Right:* David Wells's perfect game will long be remembered by Yankee fans as a magical moment.

1919: Yankees Purchase Babe Ruth

I N THE FALL OF 1919, Boston Red Sox owner Harry Frazee was out of patience. Pitcher-turned-slugging-outfielder Babe Ruth was becoming more trouble than he was worth. Although his contract had two years to go and Ruth had hit a record 29 home runs that year, he had balked at pitching and had jumped the club before the end of the season. He also set another record for late nights and carousing. Now he wanted a new, more lucrative deal. If he didn't get it, he threatened to quit baseball and become a boxer or a movie star.

Frazee, a successful theatrical producer, concluded that "the show must go on" minus Ruth. A year earlier, Yankee owner Jacob Ruppert had expressed interest in Ruth, who seemed to hit a home run every time the Red Sox played the Yankees. Frazee contacted Ruppert, and on December 26, the Yankees agreed to purchase Ruth for $100,000 and "other considerations."

The rest is history: Yankee history.

Yankee owner Jacob Ruppert (right) had no regrets about the purchase of Babe Ruth. As a Yankee, Ruth became the greatest slugger the game has ever known. Ruth's substantial salary was one of the best investments the Yankees ever made.

As a Yankee, Babe Ruth became the greatest drawing card in the history of the game. While the Yankees didn't actually mint their own coins like these, when Ruth was a Yankee the franchise virtually printed money, becoming the wealthiest franchise in the game.

1927: Ruth Hits 60th Home Run

ON SEPTEMBER 29, 1927, Babe Ruth smacked two home runs against the Washington Senators, his 58th and 59th of the season, tying his own record. Ruth had two games to set a new mark.

On September 30, just over 10,000 fans turned out at Yankee Stadium on a Friday afternoon to see if Ruth could outdo himself. The Bambino didn't disappoint.

In the eighth inning, with the score tied 2–2, Ruth came to bat against Washington pitcher Tom Zachary. Zachary had pitched well, but he had trouble with Ruth, who had already smacked two hits and scored both Yankee runs. Now, with a runner on third and the game on the line, Zachary pitched Ruth carefully.

He wasn't careful enough. With a 1–1 count, Zachary threw what Ruth later described as a slow screwball, down and in. Ruth turned on the pitch, sending it out like a rifle shot to right field. It rattled into the bleachers, just fair, as all 10,000 fans cheered and waved.

Baseball had a new record.

Ruth's 60th home run was like most of his blasts hit at Yankee Stadium—a long, soaring drive he pulled down the right-field line.

1932: Gehrig Blasts Four Home Runs

On June 3, the Yankees squared off against the Philadelphia A's in Philadelphia's Shibe Park. In order to stay in the pennant race, the A's desperately needed a win. Lou Gehrig had other ideas.

In the first inning he cracked a two-run home run to give the Yankees a quick 2–0 lead. But when he came up for the second time in the fourth inning, the Yankees trailed 3–2. Not for long. Gehrig's solo shot tied the game, but the A's stormed back to retake the lead once more in the bottom of the inning.

The Yankees rallied in the fifth, bringing up Gehrig for the third time. Boom. He drove pitcher George Earnshaw from the game with his third home run.

When Gehrig came to bat for the fourth time in the seventh, A's fans stood and cheered. Gehrig responded, driving his fourth home run of the day over the right-field fence, becoming the first player in the 20th century to hit four home runs in a game.

As the Yankees romped to an eventual 20–13 win, Gehrig had two chances to hit home run number five. After grounding out in the eighth, in the ninth inning Gehrig hit his longest shot of the day, a 450-foot fly ball. Unfortunately, the fence in center field was 468 feet away, and the ball was caught for an out.

Gehrig's powerful swing made him the second greatest slugger in baseball. Although Babe Ruth often overshadowed his teammate, Gehrig's four home runs on June 3, 1932, were unique in Yankee history. Not even Ruth hit so many home runs in a game.

1939: The "Luckiest Man" Bids Farewell

AFTER PLAYING IN 2,130 consecutive games, on May 2, 1939, Lou Gehrig removed himself from the Yankee lineup. Since spring training it had been obvious that something was wrong with the slugger. Doctors soon discovered he was suffering from amyotrophic lateral sclerosis, a deadly nerve disease.

On July 4, the Yankees held Lou Gehrig Appreciation Day at Yankee Stadium. Between games of a doubleheader, Gehrig, surrounded by his teammates, approached a microphone stand near home plate. Gehrig had prepared a farewell speech, but at the last second he told sportswriter Sid Mercer, the master of ceremonies, that he was too emotional to speak. When Mercer told the crowd, they began chanting "We want Gehrig! We want Gehrig!"

The first baseman reluctantly complied. He approached the microphone and abandoned his written words. Instead, he spoke from the heart, delivering the most famous speech in baseball history, saying, "Fans, for the past two weeks you have been reading about what a bad break I got. Yet today I consider myself the luckiest man on the face of the earth."

Gehrig wipes away tears as he tries to control his emotion while bidding farewell to baseball.

New York sportswriter Sid Mercer introduces Gehrig on Lou Gehrig Appreciation Day as his teammates look on.

1941: DiMaggio Hits in 56 Straight Games

O N MAY 15, 1941, Joe DiMaggio was off to the worst start of his major-league career and the Yankees had a record of only 14–14. Earlier that day in the *New York Herald Tribune*, sportswriter Dan Daniel wrote "When DiMaggio begins to hit again he will pull the other Yankees with him." DiMaggio responded with a hit and made solid contact in two other at-bats. Although the Yankees lost 13–1, Daniel's words proved accurate.

For the next two months, Joe DiMaggio collected at least one base hit in every game he played. As he did, the Yankees followed his lead, taking command of the pennant race.

By the time DiMaggio's hitting streak reached 45 games on July 2, breaking the existing record held by Wee Willie Keeler, Joe's quest had captured the attention of the nation. Every day fans asked each other, "Did Joe get a hit today?"

He did, running the streak to 56 games on July 16, in Cleveland. Then, on July 17, Cleveland third baseman Ken Keltner made two great plays, robbing DiMaggio of two hits. When DiMaggio grounded out to shortstop Lou Boudreau in his last at-bat, the longest hitting streak in major-league history came to an end.

Left: DiMaggio's final hit of the streak was this ground-ball single on July 16.

Right: DiMaggio celebrates after tying Wee Willie Keeler's record 44-game hitting streak. DiMaggio had a base hit off Boston pitcher Jack Wilson.

44 EQUALS RECORD

DiMaggio's record spawned another kind of record, a 78 rpm recording called "Joltin' Joe DiMaggio." It was sung by Betty Bonney, played by Les Brown and his orchestra, and written by Alan Courtney and, appropriately enough, songwriter Ben Homer.

1956: Mantle Hits 565-foot Home Run

ON APRIL 17, Yankee slugger Mickey Mantle served notice that he was at the peak of his career. On his way to winning the Triple Crown, Mantle hit what might have been the longest home run in major-league history.

The Senators were playing host to the Yankees on a sunny Friday afternoon in Washington before only 4,206 fans when Mantle, batting right-handed, stepped up to the plate in the fifth inning to face veteran left-handed pitcher Chuck Stobbs. Stobbs threw Mantle a fastball, letter-high. He swung. The ball soared toward left center field . . . and just kept going.

Helped by a gentle breeze, Mantle's blast easily cleared the fence 391 feet away, then it ticked past the football scoreboard at the back of the stands 515 feet from home plate.

Yankee public relations director Red Patterson raced out to find the ball and discovered it across Fifth Street in the

As seen on this cover story in *Life* magazine, by 1956 Mickey Mantle was one of the most popular and recognized Americans.

backyard of a house at 434 Oakdale Street. Although he claimed to have measured the blast at 565 feet, he later admitted that he merely paced the distance off. Still, although Mantle and others may have hit longer home runs, Mantle's blast is widely accepted as the longest measured home run in baseball history. It is recognized as such in the *Guinness Book of World Records.*

Although Mantle hit his 565-foot blast while swinging right-handed, he actually had more power swinging from the left side.

129

1956: Larsen Hurls Perfect Game

In 1954, WHILE PITCHING for Baltimore, Don Larsen lost 21 games. He was traded to the Yankees and was inconsistent, but in September 1956, Larsen decided to pitch without a windup. His control suddenly improved, and he won four straight games. When the Yankees made it to the World Series, Casey Stengel picked Larsen to pitch Game 2.

He was knocked out of the game, but Stengel believed in Larsen and brought him back in Game 5. In the fourth inning, Mickey Mantle hit a home run, breaking up a no-hitter by Dodger pitcher Sal Maglie and giving Larsen a 1–0 lead.

That was when many fans noticed that Larsen was also throwing a no-hitter. Mantle made a fine catch in the fifth to preserve the no-hitter, and the Yankees scored a second run in the sixth. Larsen entered the ninth inning needing only three outs to make history. Not only hadn't he given up a hit, he hadn't given up a baserunner.

Pinch-hitter Dale Mitchell was the final batter, and on his 97th pitch of the game, Larsen struck out Mitchell, becoming the first pitcher to throw a perfect game in the World Series. More than 50 years later no other pitcher has duplicated his feat.

Above: Since throwing his perfect game, Don Larsen often makes note of the accomplishment when he signs a baseball. *Left:* An ebullient Yogi Berra leaps into Larsen's arms seconds after Larsen recorded the 27th out of the ball game.

1961: Maris Hits 61st Homer

As Roger Maris chased Babe Ruth's record of 60 home runs in a single season, he faced incredible pressure. Some fans thought Maris, due to his relatively low batting average, wasn't worthy to succeed Ruth. Baseball commissioner Ford Frick didn't help matters when he announced that unless Maris surpassed Ruth in 154 games, Ruth would retain the record for a 154-game season.

Although Maris was under so much stress trying to break the record that his hair was falling out, on September 26, in game 159, he tied Ruth. But on the last day of the season he was still stuck on 60 home runs.

In the fourth inning at Yankee Stadium, he stepped in against pitcher Tracy Stallard and roped a line drive to right field. The ball rocketed into a sea of hands six rows deep, where it was caught by 19-year-old fan Sal Durante. It had taken 162 games, but Roger Maris had bettered Ruth's mark. The home run record was his.

Sal Durante, the fan who caught home run 61, poses with Maris after the game. Durante tried to give the ball to Maris, who refused it. Mantle told Durante to sell the ball. He did, selling it for $5,000 to a restaurant owner who eventually returned the ball to Maris.

Above: Only 23,154 fans were at Yankee Stadium on October 2, 1961, to witness history. Here Maris crosses home plate after hitting home run 61. *Right:* In the wake of the 1961 season, every little boy wanted to be Roger Maris. Playing this Roger Maris Action Baseball game allowed young fans to fulfill the fantasy.

1976: Chambliss Home Run Wins Pennant

THE YANKEES WON the AL East in 1976 and earned the right to play in the postseason for the first time since 1964, the longest drought they had experienced since purchasing Babe Ruth. But they still needed to beat the Kansas City Royals in the best-of-five ALCS to win the pennant.

The two teams split the first four games and were tied 6–6 when Yankee first baseman Chris Chambliss stepped to the plate to lead off the ninth inning. Royals pitcher Mark Littell left a fastball up, and Chambliss turned on the pitch, driving it deep to right field. When it landed in the stands, the Yankees were American League champions.

Well, technically, that had to wait until Chambliss crossed home plate. But as he toured the bases, hundreds and then thousands of Yankee fans poured onto the field, forcing Chambliss to run through a human obstacle course on his way home. Somewhere between third base and home the crowd closed in, and Chambliss was trapped until police found him and escorted him to the clubhouse. After the field was cleared, Chambliss went back out and officially touched home plate.

Now the Yankees were champions again.

Above: Chris Chambliss and everyone else in Yankee Stadium follow the flight of the ball after Chambliss connects. In seconds, there was pandemonium on the field. *Left:* Ecstatic fans catch up to Chambliss between second and third base as he tries to score following his game-ending home run in the ALCS .

1978: Guidry Strikes Out 18

WHILE BILLY MARTIN and Reggie Jackson battled it out over the first half of the 1978 season and the Yankees struggled, pitcher Ron Guidry emerged as a star. The little left-hander, dubbed "Louisiana Lightning," featured a potent fastball and a devastating slider that batters found almost unhittable.

When he warmed up before the game against the California Angels on June 17, he felt sluggish and told teammate Sparky Lyle that he had "nothing." But after Angels second baseman Bobby Grich led off the game with a double, Guidry suddenly settled in. His fastball had never been quicker, and his slider had never been more deceptive.

Hitter after hitter went down meekly, swinging at air as Guidry picked up one strikeout after another. By midgame, every time Guidry had two strikes on a batter, the Yankee Stadium crowd started clapping, hoping for another K.

In the ninth inning, Guidry stuck out the first two hitters to give him 18 strikeouts, the most ever by a Yankee pitcher.

And, oh yeah, he won the game 4–0.

Ron Guidry didn't look like he could throw hard, but the left-handed pitcher got everything out of his delivery. He finished the season 25–3 and won the Cy Young Award.

1979: Fans Say Good-bye to Munson

ON AUGUST 2, Yankee Captain Thurman Munson crashed his eight-seat Cessna jet while practicing takeoffs and landings and was killed. The Yankees and their fans were devastated. The next night, before their regularly scheduled game against the Baltimore Orioles, they said good-bye to the Yankee captain.

Before the start of the game, only eight players ran out to the field as Yankee catcher Jerry Narron remained in the dugout. After a prayer, opera singer Robert Merrill sang "America the Beautiful." Then, during a moment of silence, Munson's picture appeared on the scoreboard.

Without warning, the crowd at Yankee Stadium began to stir, first clapping softly, then roaring, and then cheering. They chose not to mourn Munson's death but to celebrate his life, crying and for the next eight minutes chanting "Thurman! Thurman! Thurman!" over and over again.

It was a heartfelt tribute to an unforgettable player and one of the most stirring moments in the history of the franchise.

Munson's Yankee teammates bow their heads in mourning during Munson's farewell ceremony at Yankee Stadium.

Munson's plaque in Monument Park celebrates the life of the Yankee captain. Yankee owner George Steinbrenner wrote the inscription.

1983: Righetti Pitches No-hitter on Steinbrenner's Birthday

ON JULY 4, 1983, YANKEE owner George Steinbrenner's 53rd birthday, Yankee pitcher Dave Righetti gave him a present to remember.

On a blisteringly hot day before a holiday crowd at Yankee Stadium, Righetti was in command from the start, striking out the side in the first inning and setting down one hitter after another. Although he walked several batters, everyone knew he had a no-hitter entering the ninth inning.

Jeff Newman led off with a walk, and then Glenn Hoffman hit a ground ball to short. The Yankees tried for a double play, but shortstop Andre Robertson's throw pulled Don Mattingly off the bag, giving the Red Sox an extra chance at Righetti. It did them no good.

Righetti got Jerry Remy to ground out, then he faced the toughest out in baseball, Wade Boggs, for the final out.

Righetti ended the game with style, blowing away Boggs on a 2–2 pitch like he was blowing out candles on a birthday cake. The Boss had his birthday wish, and Righetti had a no-hitter—the first by a Yankee pitcher since Don Larsen in the 1956 World Series.

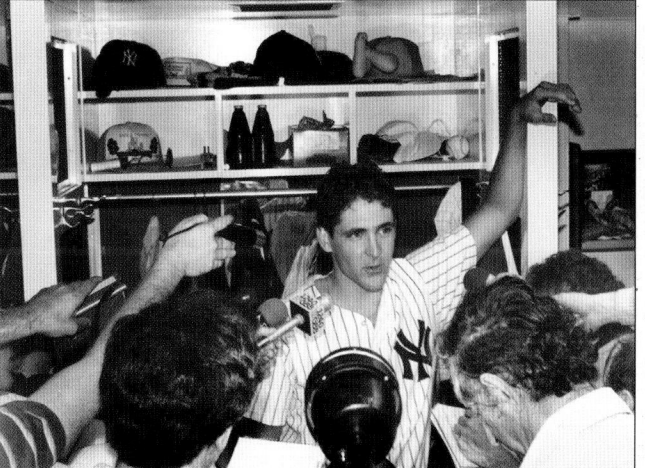

Above: Righetti, nicknamed "Rags" by his teammates, was the key acquisition by the Yankees in a trade with the Texas Rangers that sent popular relief pitcher Sparky Lyle to Texas. Here Righetti pitches the last inning of his no-hitter. *Left:* Righetti talks to the media following his gem.

1983: Martin Protests Brett's "Pine-tar" Bat

ON JULY 24, the Yankees led the Kansas City Royals 4–3. But in the ninth inning, Kansas City third baseman George Brett blasted a two-run homer off Goose Gossage to give the Royals a 5–4 lead.

At least that's what everyone thought. A moment after Brett crossed home plate, Yankee manager Billy Martin ran out onto the field and started talking with home plate umpire Tim McClelland, who then took a close look at Brett's bat.

A few weeks earlier, Yankee third baseman Graig Nettles had noticed that Brett's bat was illegally coated with pine tar. He recalled that an umpire had once taken a hit away from Thurman Munson for the same infraction. Nettles told Martin. The Yankee manager filed the knowledge away. When Brett hit the home run, Martin took action.

He explained the rule to McClelland, who measured Brett's bat, and with a flourish, called him out. Brett raced from the dugout, and one of the most famous arguments in baseball history followed.

After the game, the Royals protested the decision. Though Martin was technically correct, AL president Lee MacPhail backed the Royals and allowed the home run and the Royals win to stand.

Umpires restrain George Brett after he learns that his home run has been disallowed. In the late 1970s and '80s, Brett was known as a "Yankee killer," a player who performed best when he was playing the Yankees.

Yankee manager Billy Martin is emphatic as he argues his case with the umpires.

1996: Kid "Catches" Jeter Home Run

IN THE EIGHTH INNING of the first game of the ALCS against the Baltimore Orioles, New York trailed 4–3. With one out and nobody on, Yankee shortstop Derek Jeter stepped to the plate against Orioles closer Armando Benitez.

Jeter hit a fly ball to right field. Baltimore outfielder Tony Tarasco drifted back to the base of the wall and prepared to make the catch.

In the stands, 12-year-old Jeffrey Maier was wearing his glove, hoping for a chance to use it. As the ball came down, Maier and a half dozen fans reached and tried to catch the ball, not realizing it was still in play. The ball hit Maier's glove then bounced into the stands.

The umpire signaled home run as Tarasco pointed up and Jeter rounded the bases. Baltimore manager Davey Johnson raced from the dugout and argued that Jeter should be called out due to fan interference, but none of the umpires had seen Maier touch the ball.

The disputed home run tied the game, and the Yankees went on to win the game and the pennant. For a few days, the most famous Yankee fan in the world was Jeffrey Maier.

As if afraid the call would be reversed, Jeter circled the bases quickly after umpires signaled the hit a home run.

Young Jeffrey Maier (hatless in the black shirt) is one of several fans who tried to catch Jeter's long drive. Maier, a huge Yankee fan, later became a successful collegiate baseball player at Wesleyan University.

1998: Wells Throws Perfect Game

BEFORE HE TOOK THE MOUND against the Minnesota Twins on May 17, Yankee pitcher David Wells already had a lot in common with former Yankee pitcher Don Larsen. Both were graduates of Point Loma High School in San Diego and both had a reputation for having a little too much late-night fun off the field. They would soon have even more in common.

Two starts earlier, Wells had failed to hold a big lead and had angered manager Joe Torre by flipping the ball in the air when he was pulled from the game. Wells knew he needed a big performance against the Twins.

He got all that and more. His control was impeccable from the start, and the Yankees gave him an early lead. Wells stayed ahead of the Minnesota hitters and kept them off balance all game, going to a three-ball count only twice. No one came close to getting a hit.

By the ninth inning, everyone in the Stadium knew that Wells was not only pitching a no-hitter, but a perfect game. ESPN even broadcast the end of the game nationwide.

On Wells's 120th pitch, Pat Meares lofted a soft fly ball to right field. When it was caught, David Wells joined Don Larsen as the second pitcher in Yankee history to throw a perfect game.

Overjoyed, Wells accepts the congratulations of teammate Luis Sojo as catcher Jorge Posada races out to join the celebration.

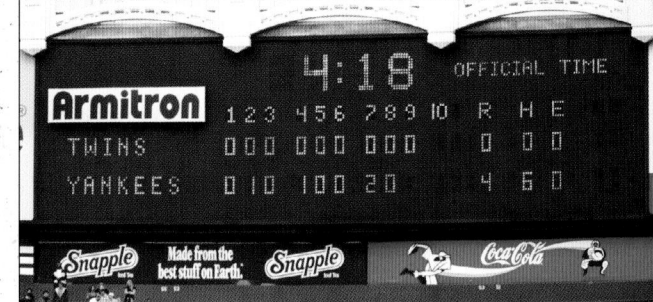

Moments after the end of the game, the scoreboard tells the story. Twins: no runs, no hits.

Wells made the front of *The New York Times* following his perfect game. No one enjoyed the attention more than the fun-loving Wells.

2003: Boone's Home Run Beats Boston

IT CAME DOWN to one swing.

In 2003, it seemed almost preordained that not only would the Red Sox and Yankees meet in the ALCS, but that the epic meeting would end in spectacular fashion.

That it did. The Red Sox appeared to have it won, leading in Game 7 with the score 5–2 after seven and a half innings before the Yankees tied the game. While Mariano Rivera held the Red Sox at bay in the 9th, 10th, and 11th innings, Tim Wakefield was just as effective for Boston, retiring the Yankees in order in the 10th. He took the mound in the bottom of the 11th and threw one pitch.

Yankee third baseman Aaron Boone was at bat. Acquired in midseason from Cincinnati, Boone had thus far been a disappointment in pinstripes. But he took one swing at a knuckleball that didn't knuckle.

Boone leaps in the air as he rounds the bases following his pennant-winning blast.

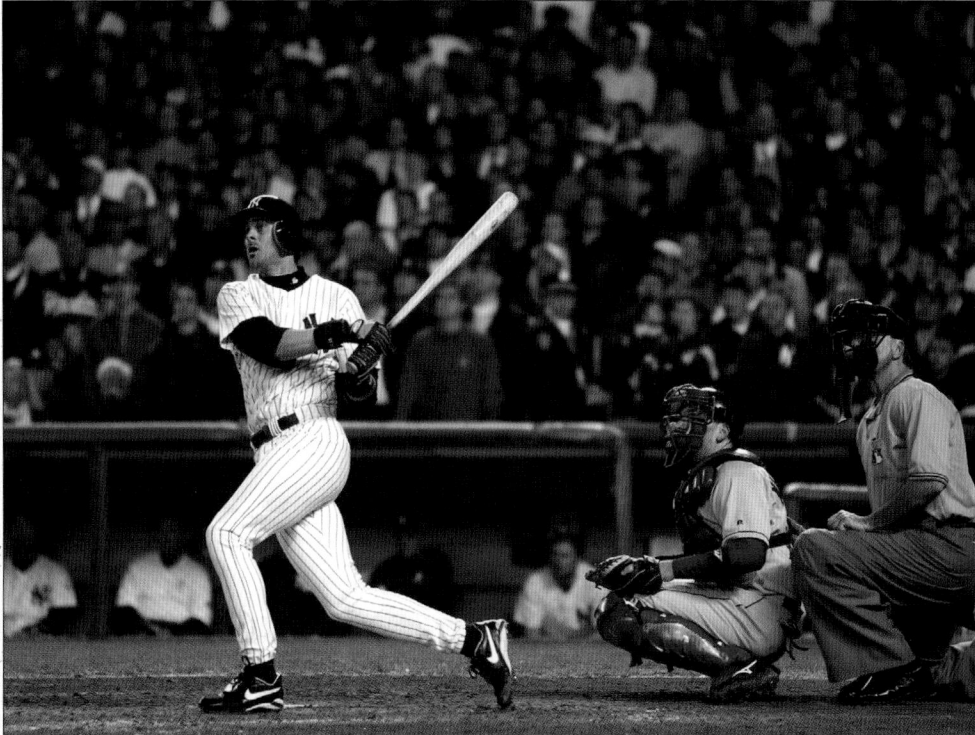

One hundred years from now, when a Yankee fan hears the name Aaron Boone he or she will think of this game-winning swing.

The ball soared toward left field, and Yankee Stadium rocked and rolled and shook as Boone raced around the bases, mouth open and arms in the air, as the ball landed far back in the left-field stands.

Put it in the book. Yankees 6, Red Sox 5, Aaron Boone famous forever.

Gehrig's Consecutive-Game Streak or DiMaggio's 56-Game Streak?

Two records have long captured the imagination of baseball fans, Joe DiMaggio's 56-game hitting streak in 1941 and Lou Gehrig's consecutive-game streak of 2,130 set from 1925 to 1939. The question of which one was more difficult is the ultimate apples or oranges question. But there is an answer.

Beginning in 1925, despite broken bones, fevers, pulled muscles, spike wounds, headaches, and other assorted hardships, Lou Gehrig played 2,130 consecutive baseball games. Although his record was bettered by Cal Ripken, Jr., in 1995, Gehrig's accomplishment came during a time when medical treatment for baseball injuries usually con-

Baseball Magazine was a popular monthly publication. Lou Gehrig was a favorite of the editors—and readers. His image was often displayed on the cover.

Gehrig didn't just play in 2,130 consecutive games—he played great. Although he occasionally left the game in late innings, Yankee fans grew accustomed to seeing Gehrig manning first base and touring the bases after a home run.

Few fans realize that DiMaggio's 56-game hitting streak was only the second longest of his career. As a member of the San Francisco Seals of the Pacific Coast League in 1933, DiMaggio hit in 61 consecutive games.

sisted of rubbing a wound with dirt, clenching one's teeth, and soldiering on. Although Ripken's record is remarkable in its own right, it is different. The fact that Ripken later surpassed Gehrig does not really figure into the argument over the two streaks.

Although Gehrig's streak is genuinely remarkable, DiMaggio's mark may well be the most difficult. Consider that since 1941 only Pete Rose, who hit in 44 consecutive games in 1978, has even come remotely close to approaching DiMaggio's mark. A streak of any kind depends on its share of good luck, but not even anyone in the minor leagues has come close to

DiMaggio. That's because DiMaggio, of all the players in the game, was somehow the best equipped to accumulate such a streak.

Not only did he hit in 56 consecutive games in 1941, and after going hitless on July 17, go on to hit in another 16 games, but in 1933, while playing his first full season with the San Francisco Seals, Joe DiMaggio hit in 61 consecutive games. This is officially recognized as the longest hitting streak in minor-league history.

What was hard for everyone else in baseball was easy for Joe DiMaggio.

DiMaggio's hitting streak made him the best-known and most admired player in baseball. Kids everywhere wanted to play like Joe, and he accommodated them with this instructional book.

Yankee Farewells

ALTHOUGH LOU GEHRIG's farewell speech and the Yankee tribute to Thurman Munson are two of the most famous farewells in baseball history, several other send-offs for former Yankees will long be remembered.

In 1946, Babe Ruth was diagnosed with throat cancer, and it became clear that he was dying. On April 27, 1947, the Yankees held Babe Ruth Day at Yankee Stadium.

Many of Ruth's ex-teammates turned out for the event. Before the game, a gaunt-looking Ruth, dressed in a heavy overcoat, stood

An obviously touched Mel Allen looks on as Babe Ruth, gaunt and dying of cancer, speaks to his fans for the last time.

No farewell in baseball history has ever evoked a more memorable moment than Gehrig's on July 4, 1939.

before a microphone near home plate and spoke to the fans.

Although his voice was hoarse and difficult to understand, Ruth rose to the occasion one last time. "The only real game, I think, in the world is baseball," he said. Ruth died the following year.

On June 8, 1969, the Yankees decided to honor another slugger: Mickey Mantle. Former Yankee announcer Mel Allen summed up the feelings of most Yankee fans when he introduced Mantle by saying, "Ladies and Gentlemen, a magnificent Yankee, number seven, Mickey Mantle."

A subdued Mickey Mantle poses with his old jersey before his retirement ceremonies on June 8, 1969.

Mantle spoke from the heart, telling fans, "To play 18 years at Yankee Stadium is the best thing that could ever happen to a ballplayer." At the end of his speech, the crowd responded with a ten-minute ovation.

Although many other Yankees have been honored with a "day" at Yankee Stadium, perhaps the most poignant farewell was completely spontaneous, delivered by Yankee fans.

After Yankee outfielder Paul O'Neill announced that he would retire after the 2001 season, he was cheered wildly during the 2001 playoffs and World Series against Arizona. When he took the field in the ninth inning of Game 5—for what seemed likely to be his last appearance in the field had the Yankees not mounted a stirring comeback to win the game—the entire crowd began rhythmically chanting, "Paul O-Nee-Ull, Paul O-Nee-Ull," refusing to stop even after the Yankee right fielder, with tears in his eyes, acknowledged the crowd.

Yankee fans' spontaneous farewell to favorite Paul O'Neill during the 2001 World Series was perhaps the most memorable in a World Series marked by one dramatic moment after another.

Index